# EXPLORING IRELAND'S HIDDEN PLACES

38 routes to discover by car

## CHRISTOPHER MORIARTY

WOLFHOUND PRESS

*To Elizabeth Healy*

---

First published 1993 by
WOLFHOUND PRESS
68 Mountjoy Square
Dublin 1

British Library Cataloguing in Publication Data
Moriarty, Christopher
    B yways Rather Than Highways: Exploring Ireland
    I. Title
    914.1504

    ISBN 0 86327 373 4 Paperback
    ISBN 0 86327 417 X Hardback

**Acknowledgements:** Grateful thanks to Elizabeth Healy who planted the idea, to Peter Harbison and Letitia Pollard who kept it watered and to all my friends in *Ireland of the Welcomes* in which the articles appeared.

The support of Bord Fáilte / Irish Tourist Board, publishers of *Ireland of the Welcomes*, is gratefully acknowledged.

Cover and book design: Jan de Fouw
Cover photograph: Jan de Fouw
Illustrations by Willem van Velzen
Map on page 4 by Eilis Ryan
Photographs on pages 68 and 82, as identified, by Jan de Fouw
Other photographs by Christopher Moriarty
Film: ten routes courtesy of Ireland of the Welcomes. Remaining separations: Pentacolour
Additional typesetting: Redsetter, Dublin
Printed in the Republic of Ireland by Colour Books, Dublin

# INTRODUCTION

Good roads connect all the well-known towns and tourist spots of Ireland.
As you pass along them at fifty-five miles an hour you will be struck by the beauty of
the surrounding land and by its variety. There is so much to see that you might
be pardoned for forgetting that, in between all those busy highways,
lies a fantastic wealth of countryside.

---

The aim of this book is to entice the traveller away from the main roads
and into those unknown in-between regions. The thirty-eight routes all
bring you from one important place to another — or maybe go on a circular tour
based on one of the cities. The main roads are avoided and the big spectacular spots
like Cashel and Killarney merit no more than a mention in passing.

---

Here you will find a wonderful choice of new ways of getting to your
ultimate destination. The routes cover the greater part of Ireland, from Mizen Head to
Inishowen. But the counties around Dublin come in for special treatment.
The fact that the author is a Dubliner might have something to do with this.
It is also true that the eastern half of Ireland, with its richer land, has been
the most populous for countless generations and therefore has the
greatest concentration of things, besides scenery, to look at.

---

The range of wonders is endless: from the concrete cows of Butler's Bridge to
the Ogham stone of Breastagh, the great cross of Clones to the lighthouse
of Hook Head, from Hell's Hole at the northernmost point of Ireland to the
fantastic cliffs of Mizen Head far to the south. There are lakes: big ones like Corrib and
Derg, small and unknown like Lough Allua. Some routes follow rivers,
others wander round about the bog. All come complete with favourite picnic spots
and places to stay or get a meal. This is a book for the person who has
a week to spend in Ireland, and for the person with a lifetime here.

CHRISTOPHER MORIARTY

## NOTES

*Planning a visit from abroad:* Contact a local office of Bord Fáilte, the Irish Tourist Board
or of the Northern Ireland Tourist Board. Or write to head offices at Baggot Street Bridge,
Dublin 2, Ireland and St Anne's Court, 59 North Street, Belfast BT1 1NB, Northern Ireland.
Make a point of asking for their brochures on private houses and other faintly offbeat
accommodation.

---

*In Ireland:* Large towns all have tourist offices open year-round, but in summer there are
temporary offices all over the country staffed by very helpful people. They are well
supplied with brochures and books with local information and will also help to find
accommodation.

---

The best maps to use on the byways are the Ordnance Survey 'Half-inch' series which
show even the smallest roads.

# IRELAND
## Primary Road Network

The locations of the *Byways* routes
described in this book are identified
here by *Route number*
(e.g. Route 4 is *The Land of the Táin*.
See contents page).
Detailed individual route maps
accompany each chapter
within the text.

Route 1

*Buncrana*

*Coleraine*

Route 2

Route 3

DERRY

*Letterkenny*

*Strabane*

*Donegal*

*Omagh*

BELFAST

*Ballyshannon*

Route 5

*Enniskillen*

*Armagh*

Route 36

*Sligo*

*Monaghan*

Route 10

*Ballina*

Route 20

Route 21

*Newry*

Route 4

Route 11

*Boyle*

*Carrick-on-Shannon*

*Cavan*

*Dundalk*

Route 22

*Westport*

*Castlerea*

Route 35

*Drogheda*

Route 13

Route 12

Route 8

Route 19

Route 18

*Tuam*

Route 9

*Mullingar*

*Athlone*

GALWAY

*Ballinasloe*

DUBLIN

*Ballyvaughan*

Route 34

Route 25

*Kildare*

Route 7

Route 38

*Portlaoise*

*Glendalough*

Route 24

Route 28

Route 37

*Ennis*

Route 29

*Carlow*

Route 6

Route 26

*Arklow*

Route 14

*Kilkenny*

Route 23

Route 30

Route 27

Route 33

*Cashel*

*Tipperary*

*Tralee*

*Kilmallock*

*Clonmel*

*Wexford*

Route 17

*Dingle*

WATERFORD

Route 32

*Killarney*

Route 31

*Lismore*

Route16

CORK

Route 15

*Bantry*

0    10    20    30 Miles

0  10  20  30  40 Kms

# CONTENTS

# BYWAYS rather than Highways
## Exploring Ireland

## 1 INCOMPARABLE INISHOWEN

*Highlights: Grianan of Aileach* colossal iron age fort with wonderful view. Pleasant summer seaside resort at *Buncrana*. Traces of ancient monastery with some of the earliest known Christian sculpture at *Fahan*. Modern fort with heavy guns and tea shop at *Dunree Head*. More early Christian sculpture and Spanish Armada relics at *Carndonagh*. *Malin Head* most northerly point of Ireland, spectacular cliffs and surf. Unique 17th century tombstone of sportsman at *Culdaff*. *Kinnagoe Bay* site of wrecking of Spanish Armada ship. One of many castles to visit at *Greencastle*. Lots of stone-age tombs and beautiful mountains in the interior of the peninsula.

*The ultimate in getting away from it all. Nestling between the great sea inlets of Foyle and Swilly, lies a region of incomparable beauty — all the more so because even the majority of the people of Ireland know relatively little about it.*

# Incomparable INISHOWEN

Paradoxically, in spite of its remoteness, there are no problems in getting there. And the natives are friendly. To prove it, a group of them planned a route 100 miles long and signposted it all the way to make the "Inishowen 100"

The starting point is on a mountain top, where one of the most splendid of the Iron Age stone forts of Ireland stands. The **Grianán of Aileach,** owes its well-preserved look to the fact that it was completely restored and rebuilt by an enthusiastic bishop towards the end of the 19th century.

The palace was fought over many times in its history until the powerful chieftains who owned it finally abandoned the hilltop in the 12th century. The view remains as wonderful as ever: westwards over the distant hills of mainland Donegal, eastwards to the Foyle and the city of Derry. Northwards are the hills of Inishowen itself.

In the foreground, below the Grianán, lies an expanse of flat and fertile land

surrounding a lake where hundreds of swans glide on the water. This is new land and a new lake, reclaimed from the sea by Dutch engineers who built dykes for the purpose in the 19th century. Our route winds its way steeply down the mountainside, to cross the plain and follow the coast through the seaside resorts of Fahan and Buncrana.

**Buncrana** is the bigger of the two, well supplied with guesthouses and good hotels. **Fahan** is of particular interest because a monastery was founded there by a rather unknown saint called Mura. The present day churchyard occupies the site of his establishment and a signpost shows the way to one of the oldest sculptured crosses in Ireland, carved with an intricate design sometime between the 7th and 9th centuries. It is more of a stone slab than a cross, with just two tiny projections in place of the arms.

The route through Buncrana leads out of the valley of the River Crana, over the hills to **Dunree Head.** The name of the headland means "the fort of the king" and it has a truly regal position, commanding the approaches to the greater part of Lough Swilly, a deep and safe anchorage.

The central part of the fort stands on a tiny promontory, cut off from the land by a deep chasm and reached by a drawbridge. Nowadays the fort is a peaceful spot, its great guns silent, things for children to climb on rather than to menace the ships of long-departed enemies. And there is a coffee shop just beside them. The fort itself now houses a museum and the walls of the cliff beneath it are a nesting place for fulmars and other birds of the ocean.

From Dunree, the route goes over the hill of **Mamore.** A long, straight, steep road climbs to a rock-strewn chasm. The story is that the people used to hurl the rocks down upon the heads of excisemen and policemen who came to raid the poitín makers. Indeed, so famed was the region for its abundance and quality that this firewater was also known as "a drop of Inishowen".

Down the hill and around the coast takes you to the heartland of Inishowen: not to any remote mountainside, but to the large and thriving town of **Carndonagh.** There you must stop and marvel at the skill and perhaps at the sense of fun of the sculptor who carved the cross and the two little pillars which now stand by the gate of the church at the top of the hill. Twelve or thirteen centuries ago, he created by bold and simple lines some of the most charming figures ever to grace an Irish place of worship. Having seen them, don't forget to look up at the church bell which still rings true, four hundred years after it came from a ship of the Spanish Armada.

Then the road goes northwards, through the lovely village of **Malin,** and on to Malin Head itself. The Head is easy to find because a tall lookout tower was built there in 1805. From this, the most northerly point of Ireland, there is a magnificent view of the coast of County Antrim and, farther in the distance, the hills of Scotland.

But don't just stand and look. At least walk a little way down the hill to watch the surf breaking and, ideally, take the cliff path westwards to see the stupendous cliffs

of Hell's Hole where the ocean boils with the ferocity of a witch's cauldron. The rock strata stand vertically, forced out of their position of rest by the collisions of continents a billion years ago.

From Malin Head the route goes southwards. It couldn't go anywhere else, sometimes following the sea cliffs, sometimes moving inland to pass through heather moor or between the lovely hedges of fuchsia, displaying their red, bell-shaped flowers in August. You might leave the signposted route at **Culdaff,** to

find the little church of Clonca where there is an unique tombstone of the 17th century, carved with a sword and a hurley stick and ball, commemorating the otherwise unknown warrior sportsman, Magnus MacOrristin.

Then go down to **Kinnagoe Bay** and look out across the sea, remembering the soldiers of the King of Spain whose ship, the *Trinidad Valencera* sank there in the fateful autumn of 1588.

After Kinnagoe, the character of Inishowen gradually begins to change. You leave the moorland and pass through fertile country, jealously guarded by past landowners who built themselves strong castles, the finest of them in the busy fishing port of **Greencastle.**

From Greencastle the signposted route is relatively straight and runs along the shores of Lough Foyle, ultimately returning to the mainland and the Grianán.

But remember that, at this stage, all you have seen is the edge of Inishowen. In the interior the beautiful mountains of Slieve Snacht, the Snowy Mountains, rise. And there are lakes and lonely walks and too many Stone Age monuments to mention. Inishowen is an experience, not just another piece of scenery.

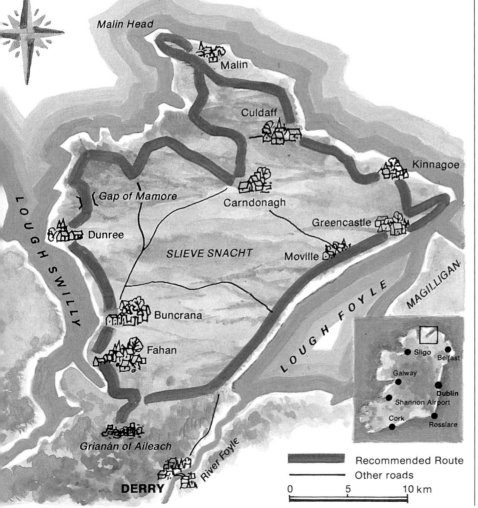

| Distances | km | miles |
|---|---|---|
| Grianán – Buncrana | 17 | 11 |
| Buncrana – Dunree | 10 | 6 |
| Dunree – Carndonagh | 29 | 18 |
| Carndonagh – Malin Head | 20 | 12 |
| Malin Head – Culdaff | 19 | 12 |
| Culdaff – Greencastle | 30 | 19 |
| Greencastle – Grianán | 36 | 22 |
| | 161 | 100 |

Inishowen is 250 km (155 miles) from Dublin. The 100 mile route needs at least two days and you could very easily spend a week there.

*Highlights:* Old seaport buildings and town houses at *Rathmelton*. Flight of the Earls heritage centre in 19th century fortress at *Rathmullan*. Specially built road to bring you to the sea and mountain scenery at *Knockalla*. Salmon farm in *Mulroy Bay*. Church with exceptional collection of contemporary artists' work in *Milford*. Colmcille heritage centre in lovely modern stone building overlooking *Gartan Lough*. Art gallery concentrating on the work of Derek Hill at his former home at *Glebe House* and a pleasant tea room, too.

*There are many byways in Donegal, indeed, highways are so rare that they qualify as attractions in their own right. One such leads into the thriving town of Letterkenny and that is a good reason for using it as the starting point for a journey.*

# Away to Fanad

A signpost for **Rathmelton** shows the way off the highway, over a hill and along the side of the great sea inlet of Lough Swilly. Rathmelton is full of surprises. The road through the village suddenly plunges down a steep hill and ends up on the quayside of a forgotten seaport. The **River Lennan** runs along the bottom of the hill and out into **Lough Swilly**, but the lough is completely hidden by steep hills so that a harbour is the last thing that anyone would expect to find there.

The quay curves gently, almost as if it was designed to display the lovely stone-built warehouses all the way along it.

Indeed it is all so picturesque that there was a real artist there on my last visit, complete with sketch pad and stool. The harbour dates to the 18th century, but there are older buildings in Rathmelton, including the first Presbyterian Meeting House ever built in Ireland and a 17th century town-house sheltering behind a large 'Take-away' sign.

A steep road, shaded by chestnut trees and bordered with ferns, leads up and away from Rathmelton and a very help-ful series of signposts saying '**Fanad Drive**' show the way onward. The next notable building is by the roadside four miles farther on and bears in large letters the words 'Brownknowe National School'. The school is so tiny, perhaps the smallest in Ireland, that its name seems to occupy most of the wall. Everything about the school is unlikely and charming: the name reflects an old song about 'The maid of the sweet brown knowe'; the building is bright with new whitewash and surrounded by a lovely flower garden with red-hot pokers and marigolds.

**Rathmullan**, the next village, is fairly steeped in history being, above all, the scene of the 'Flight of the Earls'. The earls in question, Hugh O'Neill and Ruairí O'Donnell, in 1607 sailed rather than flew to the continent and their departure marked the end of Gaelic rule in Ireland. Early in the 19th century the Government built a formidable block-house of grey-green stone to keep Napoleon out. After lying idle and un-loved for long years, this fort, now beautifully renovated, houses the 'Flight

of the Earls Heritage Centre'. You can walk the ramparts and enjoy the view across Lough Swilly to the Inishowen peninsula. Then go inside to browse amongst banners and posters and archaeological artifacts and eventually return to the fresh air: transformed painlessly to the status of expert on Elizabethan Irish life and culture.

The road after **Rathmullan** keeps close to the coast, crossing first the hill of **Lehardan** where people stop to look at the salmon farm in the sea down below, a busy place with work boats puttering here and there and silver salmon leaping in the blue water. Then comes **Knockalla**, a road constructed especially for visitors to let all who come enjoy the breathtaking scenery. The road climbs over the hills, bright with wild flowers, and at its highest point rounds a corner to give a vista of two miles and more of golden strand. When I saw it, one warm summer's day, there were nineteen people and sixty-four eider ducks enjoying the solitude. One of the greatest joys of Donegal is that there is so much space that somehow the thousands of people who holiday there never seem to make a crowd.

The turning point in the journey is **Fanad Head**, reached by a diversion signposted **Cionn Fhanaide**. There are rugged rocks and beetling cliffs, but the road leads to a lighthouse and to a lovely gentle slope of close-cropped green turf. There you can walk down to the shore or sit and gaze at the restless ocean in the general direction of Greenland. A little closer to hand, on the right, are the Scottish highlands.

From the head, the Fanad Drive takes you to **Mulroy Bay**, an inlet of the sea where, a few short years ago, modern technology finally bettered the great and good Saint Colmcille. On the shores of Mulroy an inhospitable fisherman refused to give him a morsel of the salmon he was cooking. Colmcille cursed not only the fisherman but the entire bay so that salmon were never seen there again — or not until the fish farmers set up two great rafts of sea cages wherein they swim once more in the sheltered waters.

The hills of Donegal come back into their own as you go along the edges of Mulroy: sometimes a mile or two by its stony shore, then up and down over country which closely resembles a roller-coaster, ultimately leaving the Bay at the busy town of **Milford**. The church there, a lovely white building at the apex of two avenues of red-berried rowan trees, is decorated with sculptures, stained glass and tapestries by a galaxy of the best contemporary Irish artists.

The **Fanad Drive** comes to an end at Milford. You can take a short cut to complete the circuit of the peninsula by heading for **Letterkenny**, but then you would miss the many glories of **Gartan Lough**. To find it take the road by the neat and clean **Lough Fern** to **Kilmacrenan** and turn right to follow the signpost towards **Glenveagh National Park**. The road passes an inviting cluster of thatched houses with a display of old world farm implements and coaches and an offer of tea and scones.

There are more temptations on the way, including the holy well of **Doon**

where pilgrims still come for the healing water and follow the age-old custom of tying a rag to a little bush which grows beside the well. Otherwise drive on until you meet a signpost for **Gartan** and the **Colmcille Heritage Centre**.

The saint was born close to the shores of Lough Gartan in 521 AD. Modern Gartan, quite apart from the placid beauty of the lake and the gentle hills which surround it, has much to offer. The stables of an old demesne have been beautifully restored and are used as a centre for various energetic pursuits: the lake in summer is bright with canoes and sail-boards. Close by is the Heritage Centre, a new building of stone in an ancient style. Like the Rathmullan Centre, it has a brilliantly conceived display to tell of the background and exploits of the saint and his contemporaries.

And two miles up the road, on the other side of the lake, stands another set of stables. This one contains neither canoes nor horses but an art gallery — and a tea room. The stables belong to the **Glebe House**, until recently the home of the painter Derek Hill who presented house, grounds and art collection to the nation.

Even the people of Donegal say that it rains a lot in the county. Which may be true, though the sun shines often. Whatever the weather, few remote rural regions can offer quite so much to do on a rainy day.

The round trip can be made comfortably in a day — except that all of the exhibitions deserve a few hours each.  ●

**Map legend:**
Recommended route
Other roads
0    5    10 km

Fanad Head
FANAD
Mulroy Bay
Lough Swilly
Rathmullan
Milford
Lough Fern
Rathmelton
Gartan Lough
Kilmacrenan
LETTERKENNY

Letterkenny
Sligo •     • Belfast
Galway •     ● Dublin
Limerick •
Cork •     Rosslare

| Distances | km | miles |
|---|---|---|
| Letterkenny–Rathmelton | 12 | 8 |
| Rathmelton–Rathmullan | 10 | 6 |
| Rathmullan–Fanad Head | 31 | 19 |
| Fanad Head–Milford | 31 | 19 |
| Milford–Gartan | 24 | 15 |
| Gartan–Letterkenny | 16 | 10 |
| | 124 | 77 |

A crowded beach on the Fanad peninsula — Ballymastocker Bay (Route 2).

Cliffs of basalt on the Causeway Coast, Co. Antrim (Route 3).

ABOVE: Doagh Isle on Inishowen at the northernmost extremity of Ireland (Route 1).

LEFT: The Fiddler's Stone at Castlecaldwell commemorating an 18th century musician (Route 5).

**3** ONE HUNDRED MILES OF ANTRIM COAST

*Highlights:* Well-preserved seaside castle at *Carrickfergus* and ancestral home of President Jackson. Chalk quarries at *Larne* and site of stone-age arms factory. Endless spectacular scenery, beginning with the *Glens of Antrim*. Remains of ancient lake dwelling by road to stupendous cliffs of *Fair Head*. Village of *Ballycastle* renowned for its autumn fair. Possibility of a boat trip to *Rathlin Island* where Robert Bruce studied spiders. Rope bridge to island at *Carrick-a-rede*. Ancient fort of *Dunseverick*. Highest of highlights is *Giant's Causeway* and its surrounding cliffs of basalt. Great castle of *Dunluce* and home of renowned whiskey at *Bushmills*.

*The Giant's Causeway, Killarney, and the Book of Kells are the three sweetest honey-pots of Irish tourism. If the Antrim Coast had nothing more to offer than the Causeway it would deserve a special visit. But the handiwork of the Giant is merely the supreme point of a succession of astounding scenery. The route begins in Belfast and ends at Portrush whence you may go westwards to Derry and Donegal if you don't want to go straight back to the city. Although it's less than a hundred miles (or 160 for the round trip), it needs at least one overnight because there are so many places to stop and walk around.*

# One hundred miles of ANTRIM COAST

**C**arrickfergus is the first such: almost a suburb of bustling Belfast, it somehow manages to maintain an air of tranquility belonging to a past generation. The Castle which guards the harbour is stolid and well-built — indeed it almost looks dull at first glance. Its problem is that the stone-masons who built the keep were so skilled that their work looks like new after eight hundred years. The courtyards and battlements are peopled by a pleasant assortment of ancient ordnance and modern fibre-glass figures.

If you want to make a diversion for a little American rather than Irish history, turn down the road just before leaving Carrickfergus town, to the ancestral home of Andrew Jackson, the 7th President of the United States. Otherwise continue

along the road which runs right down by the sea for most of its way.

After **Larne,** the rock formations which account for a great deal more than the scenery of Antrim make their first appearance. Larne is a busy place to this day — a convenient ferry point for Scotland and a centre for quarrying on a grand scale. The rock in the quarry is chalk which, for centuries provided lime to improve the land and to build, but with a very much longer history than that. Nodules of flint abound in chalk and the Larnian people established one of the earliest armaments businesses in Ireland with it. Eight thousand years ago

they made arrow heads and other implements and littered the seashore with their waste.

For many a mile from Larne, the sea stays on the right while on the left you pass one by one the nine **Glens of Antrim.** The glens are wide open, straight valleys cut into a plateau. The lowlands are fertile, the higher parts make an enormous expanse of moorland with little lakes and streams — enticing country if you really want to get away from it all, but it takes a long walk to reach it.

Roads go up and down each side of most of the glens and a diversion is well worth the effort. **Glenariff** is one of the finest, a broad glen with towering hills and cliffs on either side. You reach it by taking an unobtrusive turn to the left in the village of **Milltown** and there is a pleasant little restaurant at the head of the glen. The road goes back to the coast through **Waterfoot,** leaves the seaside for a while at **Cushendall** and returns to it at **Cushendun.** There, after being charmed by the Maud Cottages, a crescent of old whitewashed houses, you

embark on the Scenic Route — not that the route heretofore was anything else. It is narrow, twisty and extremely steep. You need to be prepared to be patient and hope that you don't meet a car coming in the opposite direction.

But the landscape makes it all worth while. The view is from a great height over **Torr Head** and across the ancient Sea of Moyle to Scotland. It was there that the four children of Lir, transformed to swans by a jealous stepmother, dwelt in miserable exile for three hundred years.

The road becomes easier when you pass its highest point on the shoulder of **Carnamore.** Take it very gently and give yourself plenty of time so that you can turn off first at the signpost for **Murlough Bay** where the magnificent cliffs of **Fair Head** tower above you. On the main road again, take the next turn which leads out on the Head itself. There is a lonely little lake with an island — no ordinary island but a *crannóg*, a homestead built by iron-age farmers. A walk of about a mile takes you to the Grey Man's Path, where a pillar of stone stands in a deep cleft at a terrifying height above the sea.

From Fair Head it's just a few miles down the hill to **Ballycastle,** an old seaside town where you can get a ferry to **Rathlin Island** if you are up and awake at 10.30 in the morning. There is a lovely song about the *Old Lammas Fair at Ballycastle,* celebrating its autumn festival.

Westwards of Ballycastle there are many signposts calling you to one bay or another: ideally you should stop at every one to enjoy miles of silver strand or admire the magnificent cliffs of white chalk and black basalt. **Carrick-a-rede** is one of the most exciting, famous for the rope bridge which takes you, if you are very brave, vertiginously over a chasm to a little island.

Before you reach the **Causeway** stop and look at the squat but delightful white church at **Ballintoy** and then the promontory of **Dunseverick.** The ruins there are singularly unimpressive but the legends and history make up for what they lack. It was one of the three great fortresses of Celtic Ireland: fought over by heroes, visited by Saint Patrick and finally laid waste in the 16th century.

The story that Finn MacCool built the **Giant's Causeway** so that he could walk dry-shod to Scotland pales to insignificance beside the geological facts of some of the most wonderful scenery in Ireland. The Causeway lies at the base of splendid cliffs, their forbidding blackness relieved in places by masses of red laterite rock. They represent wave after wave of lava which poured out through deep fissures in the earth's crust, filling the valleys and finally reaching the sea.

Be prepared to spend a long time there — indeed there is a big hotel and small but excellent guest houses and restaurants where you can eat and watch sea and sunset. You can walk for miles along the cliffs and also spend a long time at the National Trust's museum and information centre.

After the Causeway you might possibly feel a sense of anticlimax but the journey is far from over. A few miles along the coast is **Dunluce Castle,** a rambling medieval stronghold, so close to the clifftop that part of it actually fell into the sea some centuries ago — bringing the servants with it and totally spoiling the dinner.

And after that the lovely little town of **Bushmills,** home of one of the very best Irish whiskeys. They welcome visitors and you can see the graceful old copper pot stills. Designed many generations ago, they defy all modern high-tech attempts to produce a better drink.

At **Portrush,** renowned for golf and a sunny strand, and where religion flourishes in a bewildering variety of gospel halls, the journey ends. ●

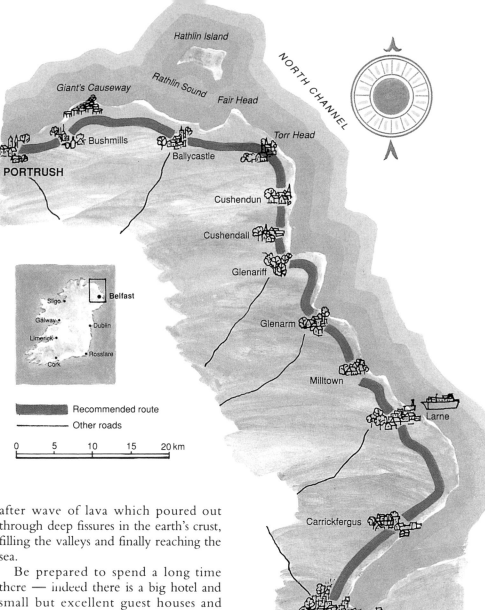

|  | miles | km |
|---|---|---|
| Belfast – Carrickfergus | 10 | 16 |
| Carrickfergus – Larne | 14 | 22 |
| Larne – Glenarm | 11 | 17 |
| Glenarm – Milltown | 10 | 16 |
| Milltown – Cushendun | 12 | 20 |
| Cushendun – Fair Head | 11 | 18 |
| Fair Head – Causeway | 17 | 28 |
| Causeway – Portrush | 8 | 13 |
|  | — | — |
|  | 93 | 150 |

# THE NORTH

## 4 THE LAND OF THE TÁIN

*Highlights: Proleek* enormous stone age dolmen and bronze age gallery grave. Picturesque fishing village at *Gyles' Quay*. Site of heroic battle of brown bull of Cooley at *The Bush*. *Carlingford* seaside with wild geese and seals and other wildlife, source of excellent oysters and village with well-preserved medieval buildings. Forest and mountain track on *Carlingford Mountain*. *Windy Gap* and *Big River* site of more of the action in the tale of Cuchulain.

*The town of Dundalk, where this route begins, celebrated its 1200th anniversary in 1989. While the written history of the region may have begun in 789, the tales of heroic doings go back for centuries earlier and are centred across Dundalk Bay on the Cooley peninsula. The sea inlet which makes one side of the peninsula was called Carlingford by the Viking settlers who founded the present town there as a trading post. The inlet is one of Ireland's very few true fjords, a deep narrow bay with a shallow opening. The round trip from Dundalk is quite short and can be done in a comfortable day out from Dublin.*

The epic story of the "driving" (the táin, pronounced "toyn") of the bull of Cooley is one of the oldest and greatest of the legends of northern Europe. It is a long story which you may read in a fine translation by the poet, Thomas Kinsella. It would be worth visiting **Cooley** just to get the feeling of the country where most of the action took place. There the hero Cúchulain defended, singlehanded, the province of Ulster from the onslaught of the men of Ireland led by the formidable Queen Medb (or Maeve).

But there is a great deal more to **Cooley** than a legend. It is a land of mountains between two sea inlets, with wonderful scenery, marvellous Stone Age tombs and, at **Carlingford,** one of the most delightful small towns in Ireland.

You find Cooley by taking the road from **Dundalk** to **Newry** and turning off at the signpost encouraging a visit to the medieval town of **Carlingford.** On the left, two miles down the road, is the Ballymascanlon Hotel which you must visit for all sorts of reasons. First, of course, you could stay there or break your journey with a cup of coffee or a meal.

It is also the beginning of the foot path which leads half a mile or so to **Proleek Dolmen.** Before you come to the dolmen, you pass a "gallery grave", a long, narrow tomb built of upright flattish stones and covered in part with a large "capstone". With a length of twelve feet, it is not surprising that this and similar graves gave rise to a legend of the giant size of our ancestors. Archaeologists and anatomists, who look at traces of bones from these ancient burials, assure us, alas, that the deceased were rather small persons.

The dolmen itself is truly magnificent, an enormous stone, estimated to weigh 40 tons, supported on three massive pillars,

standing well over six feet tall. The most remarkable fact about the two prehistoric graves is that the dolmen belongs to the Stone Age and had already stood there for a thousand years when the gallery grave was made in the Bronze Age.

After **Proleek** you take the road towards **Carlingford,** passing by a neat, colourful row of cottages built for workers on the old demesne in the 19th century. The road stays in the lowlands, with mountain to the left, sea on the right. You may make a diversion to **Gyles' Quay,** a very beautiful, utterly remote little fishing village, with a row of seven whitewashed fishermen's houses with slate roofs.

The next village with its old church and ruined school on a hill to the right, is called **The Bush** nowadays, but in ancient times was Finnabair Chúlainge. It was here that the brown bull himself was abducted by Queen Medb's followers. But he slew fifty heroes and withdrew, to the mountains, with his retinue of three score heifers.

The latter-day bulls of Cooley are less belligerent and we may proceed in safety towards the ferry port of **Greenore,** so that you go along the pleasant seaside road to **Carlingford.** In summer, it's a busy place, with sailing boats and windsurfers. In autumn, it's equally busy, but the people have been replaced by birds which have flown in from lands to the north to enjoy the mild Irish winter. Among them are small wild geese with black faces. Every year they cross the Atlantic, travelling by Iceland and Greenland, to nest in the peace and quiet of the arctic islands of Canada.

Just before coming to Carlingford (Ireland's tidiest town in 1988), you pass an oyster pond where these delectable molluscs are kept in comfort and security until big enough to be eaten. They are served, among other places, by the open turf fire in P. J. O'Hare's traditional pub-cum-grocery shop in the middle of the town. P. J. is the expert on local history and has a fine collection of pictures of Carlingford in times gone by.

The town has somehow retained its flavour of old days, with narrow streets and traces of 15th century town houses.

Look closely at one called The Mint whose stone work is decorated in a style which dates to five hundred years before the house was built. Above the harbour stands a splendid castle, its building begun about the year 1200 but added to and enlarged many times thereafter.

Travelling on from **Carlingford**, you see the **Mountains of Mourne** across the water, while you may climb the Cooley hills on the left. A signpost two miles along the road shows the way up a wonderful winding track high on the side of **Carlingford Mountain.**

The road along the side of the Lough passes first a little modern open air Calvary, then the village of **Omeath** and then a pub called Davy's. There you head into the mountains and reach the Long Woman's Grave. A plaque tells how she came from Spain and died of despair when she saw the poverty of the surrounding land. She clearly had no eye for beauty and, indeed, little enough of a judgment of land because you can see to the north, from a pinnacle above her grave, a lovely landscape of fertile fields in County Down.

The maps call this place the **Windy Gap** and there is little need to quarrel with that, except that the older name was more romantic: this is Bearnas Bó Cuailnge, the Gap of the Bull of Cooley. From the gap, the road runs by the side of the **Big River.** This was the River Cronn

in the old saga and it played an active part in coming to the aid of Cúchulain, from time to time rearing up and destroying warriors by the dozen.

Cúchulain won his fight and there was peace in Ireland for many a year after that. Peace is what prevails on Cooley — go and enjoy it.

The route is an easy day's journey beginning and ending in **Dublin.** But there are several enticing places to stay and miles of mountain routes to walk — a walking route called The Táin Trail has been signposted. •

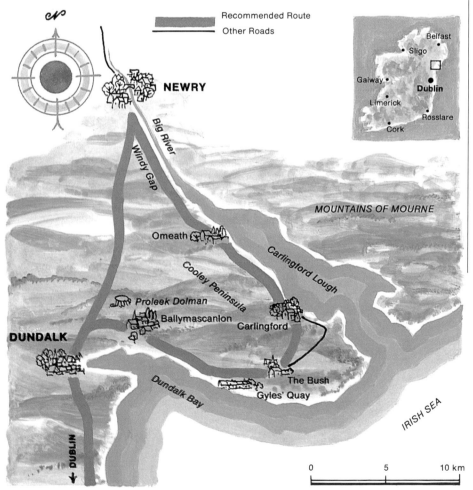

| Distances | miles | km |
|---|---|---|
| Dundalk – Ballymascanlon | 4 | 6 |
| Ballymascanlon – The Bush | 7 | 11 |
| The Bush – Carlingford | 5 | 8 |
| Carlingford – Omeath | 4 | 7 |
| Omeath – The Windy Gap | 5 | 8 |
| Windy Gap – Dundalk | 18 | 29 |
| Total | 43 | 69 |
| Dublin – Dundalk | 53 | 85 |

**5** ALONG THE WINDING
BANKS OF ERNE

*Highlights:* Border town of *Ballyshannon* with grave of the poet William Allingham. Lonely lake of *Assaroe* with woodland shores. Renowned pottery, pottery museum and restaurant at *Belleek* overlooking the river. Fiddler's stone memorial to an 18th century musician at *Castlecaldwell*. Iron-age stone idol in cemetery on *Boa Island*. Mysterious early Christian sculptures on *White Island*. Magnificent park of *Castlearchdale* with food, folk museum, collection of rare sheep and cattle and lovely walks by the shores of Lough Erne. Monastic island of *Devenish* with round tower. Wandering road amongst lakes and up the mountains at *Gortalughany*.

# Along the winding banks of Erne

*The lifestyle of the River Erne is altogether admirable. It makes a leisurely journey through the north midlands, always ready and willing to take a diversion and devote a lot of time to exploring the countryside a long way off its course. It spends its maturity in deep and placid reflection in Lower Lough Erne before taking one wild last fling over the rapids to meet the sea at Ballyshannon where our journey begins.*

**Ballyshannon** claims one of the steepest streets in any Irish town. This makes the footpaths especially pleasing, bringing you up the hill past the shops by alternating steps and level patches of pavement. This uphill journey leads to the grave of the poet William Allingham who was buried there in 1889. The churchyard where he lies gives a marvellous view down over the Erne and its once busy harbour and away south to the mountains and westwards to the ocean. In less peaceful times Ballyshannon was a place of the greatest strategic importance, commanding the river which effectively cuts Donegal off from the rest of Ireland.

From Ballyshannon there are – or at least there were – two roads to **Belleek.** The northern one, alas, has long been blocked but it is well worth taking it as a diversion. It is quite well hidden but there is a signpost which says **Knader Wood Scenic Drive.** This leads you close to the shore of **Assaroe Lake,** a faintly misleading name since Assaroe means 'the red waterfall'. There was indeed a waterfall there until the

Electricity people built two dams and hid it. The lake, though man-made, is delightful and the road wanders in and out amongst its islands. After which you must turn back and cross the Erne by the fine arched bridge in Ballyshannon.

**Belleek** is where they have been making wonderful ornamental china since 1857. The pottery is in a big, three-storey stone building on the banks of the Erne and is a

lovely place for a visit. They have, as you might expect, a museum and a splendid showroom but for good measure they add a riverside park and a very tempting restaurant and serve you off their own pottery.

Five miles farther on in an old wood is the gate of **Castlecaldwell.** The gate lodge is old and so are the trees and you might almost drive past it without noticing the stone fiddle which stands there. It was carved in tragic circumstances more than two hundred years ago and commemorates the

musician Denis McCabe who fell out of a barge nearby. Sound advice is cut beneath his epitaph:

Beware ye fiddlers of ye fiddlers fate, nor tempt ye deep least ye repent too late.
Ye ever have been deemed to water foes: then shun ye lake till it with whiskey flows.
On firm land only exercise your skill/there may ye play and drink your fill.

The castle is in a sorry state, but enough remains to testify to the wealth and power of the Caldwells who built it in the 17th century, overlooking **Lough Erne.** Many footpaths allow you to walk amongst the ancient lichen-covered trees.

**Boa Island** is the next place to stop, taking a right turn three miles farther on. After passing the car park proceed for a mile and a quarter and stop at the signpost for Caldragh Cemetery. Walk down the concrete path on the right which leads past a farm to an old cemetery. There you will meet one of the rarest stone figures in the countryside. It – or he – is a two-faced person, boldly carved with arms crossed in a way that make him look as if he holds a pair of Indian clubs. He is one of very few iron age idols or perhaps totem figures which survived the enthusiastic iconoclasm of the early Christians. He has a companion nowadays, a smaller figure from the nearby **Lustymore Island.**

Back on the mainland from Boa Island you might be tempted to head for **Pettigo** and thence to **Lough Derg,** hidden away amongst the barren hills of Donegal and in summer a very busy place of pilgrimage where people spend a night of vigil, prayer and fasting.

The lakeside road passes by **White Island** which, like Boa Island, has a collection of unique sculptured figures. These are Christians, apparently carved some centuries after the idol but sharing with him the same sharp delineation and also the fact that there

is nothing else in Ireland quite like them. Boats for White Island ply from the marina in the great estate of **Castlearchdale** which is the next definite stopping place – there are several tempting lay-bys and woodland parks on the way.

The driveway to the **Visitor Centre** goes through green, rolling parkland with magnificent trees. The great 18th-century house has gone, but its magnificent court-yard remains and is packed with old farm machinery, exhibitions to explain the abundant wildlife and a museum to com-memorate the use of Castlearchdale as a key seaplane base during World War II. Nearby a fenced paddock encloses a collection of rare breeds of cattle, goats and sheep. You would be very wise to spend a day at Castlearchdale and you can get meals there, too, in summer.

Before you come to the town of **Enniskillen,** which straddles the land between Upper and Lower Lough Erne, there is a signpost to the right where your road meets a main road on the left. This shows the way to a boat for **Devenish,**

yet another of the illustrious islands of the lake. Devenish has a round tower and other remains of a great monastery.

From Enniskillen, take the main road for **Belfast** as far as **Lisbellaw** where a signpost to **Carry Bridge** takes you off amongst green fields and hilly lands back to the Erne where the river loses itself amongst innumerable islands. Carry Bridge, once a remote crossroads, is a busy river port now where pleasure cruisers tie up and where there is a small hotel. The road passes small lakes and large, eventually taking you to **Florence Court,** a great

house in incomparable surroundings and, as a property of the National Trust, in-viting you to come and admire it at a modest fee.

One more diversion before crossing the border near **Swanlinbar** is a signpost to **Gortalughany Viewing Point,** an extremely narrow and steep road which brings you high on the heather slopes to gaze down over Lough Erne and its islands.

South of Swanlinbar take a left turn for **Ballyconnell** where they are busy rebuilding the canal which connects the Shannon and the Erne, Ireland's two greatest waterways. Then head for **Mill-town** and a diversion to **Drumlane Church;** half a round tower and a big, but singularly drab, ruin of a church, yet a heavenly setting on a hill above a sheltered arm of Lough Erne where wild duck live in peace amongst the reeds.

After Milltown come **Killykeen** and **Killeshandra** and **Kilmore** and so to **Cavan** town. Any or all of them worthy of visit - you can read all about them on page 52.

Distances

|  | Miles | km |
| --- | --- | --- |
| Ballyshannon – Assaroe | 5 | 8 |
| Assaroe – Belleek | 10 | 16 |
| Belleek – Castlearchdale | 21 | 34 |
| Castlearchdale – Carry Bridge | 18 | 29 |
| Carry Bridge – Florence Court | 8 | 13 |
| Florence Court – Milltown | 22 | 35 |
| Milltown – Cavan | 18 | 29 |
| Total | 102 | 164 |

## 6 BYWAYS OF EAST CLARE

*Highlights:* Busy riverside town of *Killaloe* with ancient cathedral and churches, associations with King Brian Boru. Old castle and new reconstructions of prehistoric Celtic dwellings in a hidden valley at *Craggaunowen*. Not quite so old castle on a hill at *Knappogue*, more a stately home open to visitors and offering 'medieval banquets'. Romantic ruins of friary at *Quin*. Iron age royal site at *Magh Adhair*. Ancient and modern town of *Ennis*. Lakeside village of *Corofin* with heritage centre, on the edge of the Burren. *Dysert O'Dea* with castle and tea and a unique celtic cross. On the way back to Limerick the far-famed castle and folk park of *Bunratty*.

*Scones like my mother used to bake are served beside the lake in the woodland cottage of Craggaunowen. It would be worth travelling a long way just for that. But Craggaunowen is the most charming as well as the most interesting of a host of things beautiful and historical in East Clare.*

# Byways of East Clare

You can journey there by a wandering way beginning in the city of **Limerick**. Look out for signposts to **Killaloe** and **Lough Derg**. These guide you across the **River Shannon** northwards to Killaloe, one of the most attractive riverside towns in Ireland. High hills of slatey rock rise on each side of the town: the rock is so hard that it dams the river making it spread out a few miles upstream to form Lough Derg, one of the biggest lakes in the country.

And that in turn made Killaloe a place of the greatest strategic importance in days gone by. The chieftains of the ancient kingdom of Thomond dwelt there and endowed the early Christian church so generously that many great and good saints settled. As you approach the town from Limerick, the first major building is the graceful gothic cathedral of St. Flannan. Beside it in the churchyard is a very much more ancient church, about nine hundred years old and notable for its stone roof.

A little way to the north of the town stands the tall, steep-sided earthen fort of Béal Boru, associated with the great king Brian who fought and perished in the Battle of Clontarf in 1014.

The road stays close to the Shannon and runs along by the side of Lough Derg before climbing high on a ridge at Ogonelloe. Then you go downhill to **Tuamgraney** where a signpost points to **Ennis** and leads you off amongst fields and hedges and small lakes. Try to go there in July when the cream-coloured flowers of elder brighten the hedges and the scent of new-mown hay brings back an almost lost age of unmechanised farming.

Turn left in **Bodyke**, keeping to the Ennis road and then watch out for the first of the signposts to **Craggaunowen**. The signposts are very important because the 'project' has yet to get its name printed on the maps. The narrow road goes by a broad, shallow lake and then into a deep valley with a view of a tall castle on a hill to the right.

This was the only ancient building on the spot and was refurbished as a home and museum by the antiquarian, John Hunt, who conceived the **Craggaunowen Project**. The idea was to reconstruct typical dwellings from Ireland's distant past, using the discoveries of archaeologists as a guide. So you may go and see what the Iron Age lake dwellings or 'crannógs' looked like, feel how it might have been to live in a ring fort, scramble through a souterrain and so forth.

A very modern exhibit is the wood-and-leather boat in which Tim Severin and his companions crossed the Atlantic. He followed the route of St. Brendan the Navigator and showed that the saint could have reached the promised land of America centuries before the Vikings.

There are people to watch, too, young craft workers using ancient methods of spinning, weaving and dyeing wool or a thatcher renovating the roofs of the buildings with the long, straight stems of reeds from the lake. And then there is the reception cottage for that cup of tea and scones.

But there is something more to Craggaunowen. The buildings of the Project nestle in a hidden valley. In the centre is a lake with lilies and wild duck and reeds. All around, the hills are clothed with birch and pine trees, with moss-covered rocks on the woodland floor. Go there when it opens at ten in the morning, before your fellow visitors, and wander in peace and solitude.

Outside Craggaunowen, life continues at an old world pace. The roads are much too narrow and twisted to allow anyone to do anything in a hurry. Turn right as you leave and follow the next set of signposts for **Knappogue**.

The castle there is a world away from Craggaunowen: for the latter you plunge down into a valley, for Knappogue you take a broad pathway up a hill, amongst green fields and rare black sheep. The central castle was built by security-conscious landowners in the 15th century. Knappogue, however, was embellished in the 19th century and became the centre of a landlord's mansion. Dead and decayed by the 1950s, it was restored on a magnificent scale by a family from Texas. If you visit it in the daytime you may wander at will to look at the furniture and admire the garden and scenery. At night you may feast yourself at a 'Medieval Banquet'.

A left turn from Knappogue leads to **Quin** with its splendid ruined friary still standing proudly and romantically amongst green fields beside a clear stream. The friary was built in 1433 within the ruins of a much older castle. You can still see the foundations of its ancient towers.

At the gate of the friary is the first of three signposts in the village leading towards **Magh Adhair**. They take you to a narrow lane and over a stream by an old stone bridge. The site is a flat-topped mound, surrounded by a ditch and topped by hawthorn bushes. Magh Adhair is well known in history as the place where the

kings of Thomond went through their inauguration ceremony. Brian Boru himself was crowned there.

The lane leads back to the road to Craggaunowen. Turn left and left again at the next crossroads for the busy town of **Ennis.** It has excellent hotels and many historical buildings. From Ennis a road leads northwards to **Corofin,** a pleasant village in the middle of a fabulous land of lakes. The former Protestant church there has been opened as the 'Clare Heritage Centre', with a very good exhibition of 19th century life in the region. You may browse amongst books and trace your ancestry there, too.

Three miles south is **Dysert O'Dea** with yet one more castle and teas. Near the castle stand the ruins of a monastic settlement, with a particularly fine high cross: not the typical 'celtic cross' but a much rarer sort with almost life-sized

figures. In the old church nearby is a wonderful romanesque doorway, decorated with curious human faces. Each one is different and they may have been portraits.

Then the great problem is where to go. You can return to Ennis and a fast road to Limerick, passing **Bunratty Folk Park** and its famous castle. But at Corofin you are on the edge of **West Clare** and that is a region so strange and beautiful that you would be crazy to miss it. ●

East Clare distances

|  | km | miles |
|---|---|---|
| Limerick – Killaloe | 17 | 11 |
| Killaloe – Tuamgraney | 13 | 8 |
| Tuamgraney – Craggaunowen | 18 | 11 |
| Craggaunowen – Magh Adhair | 11 | 7 |
| Magh Adhair – Corofin | 27 | 16 |
| Corofin – Ennis | 14 | 9 |
| Ennis – Bunratty | 17 | 11 |
| Bunratty – Limerick | 11 | 7 |
|  | 128 | 80 |

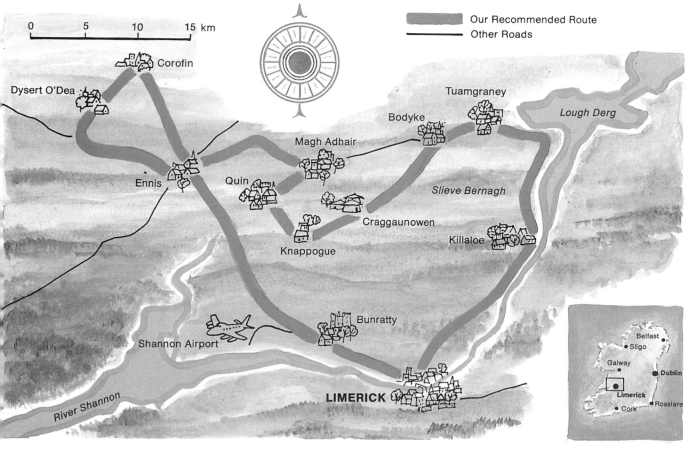

**7** EXPERIENCING THE BURREN

*Highlights:* Landscape is *the* highlight of the Burren: grey stone desert relieved by sheets of many-coloured wild flowers. One of the greatest iron age forts is at *Cathair Chomain* and stone age tomb nearby. Dramatic ruins of the historic *Lemaneh Castle*, home of the formidable Maire Ruadh O'Brien. Burren Display Centre at *Kilfenora* and nearby cathedral with medieval sculpture. Busy spa town of *Lisdoonvarna* with hotels and restaurants. Castle at *Ballynalacken* and coast road after it, with fine view of the Aran Islands. Welcoming cavern and visitor centre at *Ailwee Cave*. One of the best known dolmens at *Poulnabrone*.

*The Burren is an experience. Almost a desert, but not quite, its bare grey rock is studded with little patches of green grass or mysterious woods of hazel and everywhere there are wild flowers. That alone would be enough to make a visit well worth while. But, amongst the rocks and flowers, Stone Age tombs are scattered far and wide together with castles and cathedrals and lakes and caves. There is nothing quite like it in Ireland, nor anywhere else in the world.*

# Experiencing the BURREN

You approach **the Burren** from the everyday surroundings of **Limerick** and **Shannon** by going through **Ennis** to **Corofin** whence you follow the road for **Lisdoonvarna.** As you proceed, passing the lovely **Inchiquin Lake,** the landscape towards the north gradually changes from the familiar green fields and hedges to a region more and more dominated by stone. After the village of **Kilnaboy,** a signpost on the right indicates **Cathair Chomain** and provides an opportunity to plunge into deepest Burren

and immerse yourself in a lonely spot, away from the majority of your fellow tourists.

A narrow little road winds its way up the hill, between stone walls. Look carefully at the intricate patterns of these walls (when you reach a safe parking place), built without mortar of angular lumps of rock, gathered from the hillside where a helpful glacier dumped them ten thousand years ago.

Two signposts greet you about a mile up the road. On the left there is a Wedge Tomb, on the right a 'Viewing point East Burren'. Go and look at both of them. The wedge tomb is a sort of box, its sides and covering made of enormous slabs of the local limestone. It is one of many in the Burren and was built by an affluent farmer four thousand years ago. At that time much of the Burren land was covered with a thin layer of fertile soil. Unfortunately, for the farmers, but happily for modern people in search of wilderness, the soil was a little too thin to survive agriculture for long. So it was swept away and left the grey rock surfaces.

The signpost to the right shows the way to the edge of the hill, passing an enormous boulder, one of the ice-dumped stones which was just a little too big to be built into a wall. Miles and miles of Burren present themselves, above all a great sweep of down-folded rock strata, testi-

fying to a day in the remote past when the crust of the earth sagged a little.

Back on the road, about a mile farther on, the next pointer to **Cathair Chomain** leads along a little track to a parking space beside ancient farm cottages. There you take to your feet, following a stony path, passing on the way a little hazel grove where wild orchids and ferns enjoy the cool shade. Finally the Cathair presents itself, concentric rings of great stone walls arranged in a semi-circle whose outer defence is the precipitous wall of a deep chasm. People lived there in security in the Iron Age. Now it is a place for meditation, its ground carpeted with mosses and the exquisite white star-like flowers of rare saxifrages.

Turn right when you meet the main road and drive westwards past **Leamaneh Castle,** the ruin of the great house where Maire Ruadh lived in the turbulent days of the 17th century. Her descendants agree with serious historians that she never threw her third husband out of one of his beautiful windows.

Now that you have seen a goodly share of Burren you might pay a visit to the Burren Display Centre in **Kilfenora** to buy books and postcards and maybe take half an hour to see the display and listen to a talk about the district. The Centre has taken over the old village school house and everybody there is full of enthusiasm about the region and ready to answer your questions. Don't miss the ruined cathedral next door with its delightfully sculptured high cross.

Then away through **Lisdoonvarna** which doesn't quite belong to the wilderness but does have lots of good shops and hotels and restaurants and various kinds of entertainment. The reason for its existence is that there are mineral springs and you can indulge in all sorts of health treatments if you feel so minded — but I prefer the wide open spaces and the pure air of the Atlantic which you come to just a few miles down the road, following signposts for **Fanore** and **Black Head.**

At **Ballynalacken** a noble ruined castle stands on a cliff top and beside it is a pleasant guest house. Farther on you come to the coast road and there you will find a little farmhouse with an enticing notice announcing the sale of soup. Be enticed and sit on a bench outside to watch the ocean and enjoy heavenly home-made scones with a cup of tea.

Stop anywhere along the way, get out of the car and walk for a hundred yards or a mile or as much as you like over the pavement-like stone fields amongst the wild flowers: mountain avens and rock rose and saxifrages and the delicate blue gentian, the most beautiful of all the Burren rock-garden: particularly satisfying because it is seldom plentiful and so a special reward for those who search carefully.

Two miles north of the village of **Craggah** a signpost on the right saying 'Hostels' takes you along by the only visible river in the Burren (all the others flow in underground caverns) to the ruined church of **Fermoyle.** That is where the **Green Road** begins, one of the most wonderful footpaths in Ireland, leading for miles over the hills, amongst the flowers all the way back to Ballynalacken.

But if you don't feel that energetic, keep to the coast road around **Black Head** and so into **Galway Bay** with a view of the distant hills of Connemara.

**Ballyvaughan** is a busy village with a harbour and lots of cottages to rent. There you can turn southwards following the signposts to **Aillwee Cave.** Even if you don't want to be led by very knowledgeable and helpful young people into the bowels of the Burren, you should drive up the hill to admire first the view and then the visitor centre, a brilliant piece of architecture in keeping with the rugged surroundings. They have heaps of good souvenirs and serve outstandingly delicious snacks.

After Aillwee the road back towards **Kilfenora** and **Corofin** goes over the hills, passing many an ancient tomb and settlement before it brings you to **Poulnabrone,** where stands the dolmen that graces postcards sold throughout the length and breadth of Ireland. Don't let its over-exposure discourage you from stopping and looking and communing with the spirits of four thousand long years ago who built it when the Burren was green all over.

That was one route through the Burren. There are many more roads and many more footpaths, a places to immerse yourself in for days and days. The wild flowers are at their very best in May, but brilliant nearly any time. There is a very special map of the district, compiled by T. D. Robinson and packed with information — don't go without it.

• • • • • • • • • • • •

| Distance | km | miles |
|---|---|---|
| Limerick – Corofin | 51 | 32 |
| Corofin – Cathair Chomain | 9 | 6 |
| Cathair Chomain – Kilfenora | 13 | 8 |
| Kilfenora – Lisdoonvarna | 7 | 4 |
| Lisdoonvarna – Black Head | 19 | 12 |
| Black Head – Aillwee | 10 | 6 |
| Aillwee – Corofin | 22 | 14 |
| Round trip from Corofin | 131 | 82 |

A comfortable day's outing. ●

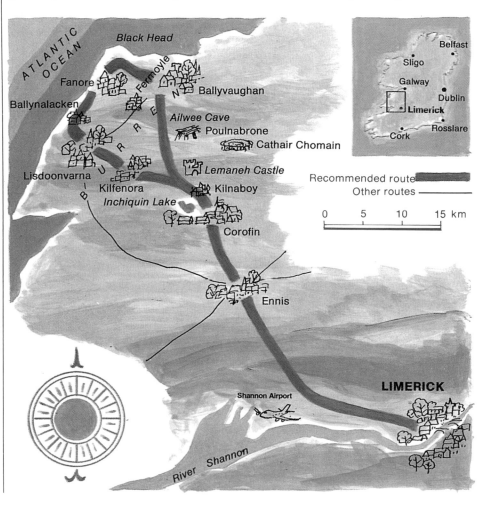

ABOVE: In the Burren limestone
land of County Clare (Route 7).

RIGHT: A waterfall at Westport.

OPPOSITE: The doorway of
Clonfert Cathedral, one of the
masterpieces of Irish 12th
century sculpture (Route 8).

*Highlights:* Roads winding their way between green hills and lakes in south *Co. Clare* (see Route 6). Lakeside villages and towns along *Lough Derg*. A peak of perfection in 12th century Irish sculpture at *Clonfert*. Broad, slow and peaceful *River Shannon* near Clonfert; followed by miles and miles of moorland. Stately home of *Clonalis*, seat of the descendants of the kings of Connaught. Town of *Boyle* and *Lough Key Forest Park* (see Route 35). Slightly inaccessible stone-age tombs of *Bricklieve Mountains*. Long lost entrance to the Celtic otherworld in *Caves of Kesh*. Visitor-friendly stone-age tombs at *Carrowmore*.

*The journey from Shannon to Sligo is a very, very long one, five thousand years and more. At the beginning you fly into that very comfortable and modern airport and at the end you may walk amongst stone monuments which were old when the pyramids of Egypt were being built. Between these extremes lie miles of meandering roads amongst green fields, purple moorland and sparkling lakes.*

# SHANNON to SLIGO

Driving northwards from **Shannon,** you leave the 20th century behind and it remains at a respectful distance for most of the trip. Our route crosses the busy main road from Shannon to **Limerick** and then loses itself in the hills, gentle green hills with tiny lakes amongst them. At **Sixmilebridge** you should begin to think of making your first stop by following the signposts to **Craggaunowen.**

With its splendid castle on a crag, towering over a lake and an ancient hazel wood, with moss-covered stones, Craggaunowen has been a wonderful spot for generations. But that isn't the half of it. The valley now contains a great open-air museum where young people work at ancient crafts. And they serve the most excellent home-made teas.

If you can resist the temptation to visit the endless conglomeration of castles and abbeys and things which surround Craggaunowen, you may proceed to **Tulla** and then go eastwards to **Lough Derg,** perhaps stopping for a picnic beside the beautiful little lake called Bridget, which lies on the right.

You meet Lough Derg close by **Scarriff,** a village with the best food to be bought for miles around. At **Mountshannon,** one of the most picturesque villages in Ireland, the road leaves the lakeside, though you might be tempted towards the

water by one of the many signposts which say "Fishing" and lead down to tiny, reed-fringed bays where nobody will disturb you.

**Portumna** is the next town and an excellent place to break the journey, to wander amongst the deer and along the lake shore in the silent forest nearby and perhaps to take a meal or stay overnight. You leave by the road which goes northwards beside the church on the main street. Here you first follow signposts to **Ballinasloe** and then for **Eyrecourt,** not

an especially important village, except that it stands on a road which goes to nowhere, but passes on its way the fantastic cathedral of **Clonfert.**

If you associate cathedrals with grandeur, you are in for a disappointment at Clonfert. The building is small and grey and rather ill-proportioned, with a tower which looks as if it doesn't quite belong. The fantasy lies in the sculpture of the doorway, part of a 12th century development. The arches are adorned with the heads of wonderful beasts, with long snouts and enormous eyes. Above the arches is a pointed hood, decorated with human heads, of which no two are the same.

The road past Clonfert doesn't really go to nowhere, in fact it leads you to the Shannon: to a remote part of that beautiful river, almost devoid of houses and inhabited only by patient fishermen concealed beneath big, bright umbrellas, who catch large numbers of small and uneatable fish. They are not natives of the place, but come for the peace from busy English industrial cities.

From Clonfert you must retrace your road a little way, before heading through Ballinasloe in the direction of **Tuam.** Moorland, beautiful in August when the purple heather is in flower, alternates with grassland, divided into fields by stone walls. The next stopping place is **Mount Bellew Bridge,** a market town with a pleasant little wood with a deerpark and a rather overgrown lakelet where swans live amongst the reeds. The people of Mount Bellew are rather coy about their wood and you have to look carefully for the signpost which shows the way to it, just outside the village.

You leave the Tuam road at **Moylough** and wander northwards to **Castlerea** which is festooned with signposts for **Clonalis,** one of the most interesting of the great houses of Ireland open to the public. It is the home of the O'Conor family, descendants of the kings of Connacht and one of the two clans which can make a legitimate claim to be *the* royal family of Ireland. It is very much an ancestral home, abounding with family portraits and with a lovely library of books and documents going back for many centuries.

The next town, **Boyle,** and the region to its north-east deserve a visit to themselves, to see the ruins of the great Cistercian monastery and to wander through the

woods and by the lakeshore of **Lough Key Forest Park.** But to continue on the byways to **Sligo,** you turn off to the left, following the signposts to **Ballymote** and climbing up and over the gentle **Curlew Mountains.** At the top of the ridge, you suddenly break out of the forest to be greeted by an extraordinary landscape. To the right lie the **Bricklieve Mountains,** flat topped with deep clefts and gulleys, green with a sprinkling of dark hawthorn bushes. Stone Age tombs abound on the summit and the view is fantastic. But access is difficult and we will take an easier route, passing beneath the fabulous **Caves of Kesh.**

Seventeen caves form a row of dark openings in a grey cliff. Some are enormous, yawning caverns, others little more

than slits. In the 19th century, scientists discovered the bones of many wild beasts, extinct in Ireland for thousands of years. There were human remains, too. From pre-Christian times, festivals have been held below the caves — which are undoubtedly the abode of infernal spirits. Celebrations are still held there on Garland Sunday, the last Sunday in July.

The road takes you through Ballymote to the main road from **Galway** to **Sligo** which you follow until the final byway, just beyond the great bay of **Ballysadare.** Follow the signpost to **Strandhill** and turn right at the new church at a crossroads on the hillside. About a mile down the road at the riding stables you may stop and study the poster and map which tell of the marvels of **Carrowmore.**

If you are tied to your car, drive a hundred yards down the road and look to the left to see a dolmen, look behind for a stone circle and to the right for a passage grave. In the distance, on top of the dramatic mountain of **Knocknarea,** is the great stone passage grave known as **Queen Maeve's Tomb.**

But it would be wrong just to drive past. Instead, you can walk over the fields, coming on some new tomb in just about every one of them. Recent excavations pushed the date of the earliest graves back to 3,000 BC: centuries before the Egyptians built their pyramids.

Just down the hill lies the busy and very hospitable town of **Sligo:** the end of the journey, but the gateway to much of the most spectacularly beautiful scenery of Ireland. ●

| Shannon-Sligo distances | km | miles |
|---|---|---|
| Shannon – Craggaunowen | 18 | 11 |
| Craggaunowen – Portumna | 61 | 38 |
| Portumna – Clonfert | 23 | 14 |
| Clonfert – Mount Bellew Bridge | 49 | 31 |
| Mount Bellew Bridge – Castlerea | 42 | 26 |
| Castlerea – Boyle | 27 | 17 |
| Boyle – Caves of Kesh | 15 | 9 |
| Caves of Kesh – Sligo | 31 | 19 |
| Total | 266 | 165 |

One day is enough for the direct journey: two or three, stopping at Portumna and perhaps Boyle would allow a thorough exploration.

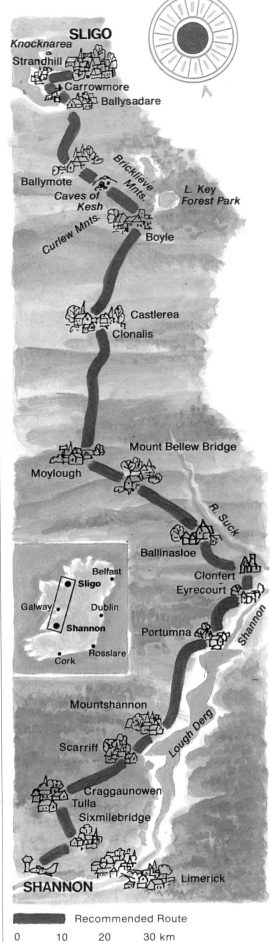

Recommended Route

0    10    20    30 km

## 9 CORRIB COUNTRY

*Highlights:* Connemara marble available in great variety at *Moycullen*. Traditional ways of farming in progress on the way to lake harbour of *Knockferry*. Beautifully restored medieval castle of *Aughnanure* with lovely surroundings. Busy town of *Oughterard*, close to lakeshore and enticing one-way drive by the lake to the *Hill of Doon*. Drive through the lake-studded moorland of *Connemara*, over the hills and down to the *Maam Valley* with romantic island castle. The canal that never was at *Cong*, then a fine old abbey and luxurious hotel *Ashford Castle* with park overlooking the lake. More old abbeys at *Headford* and *Annaghdown* and Irish-speaking village of *Menlough*.

*Lough Corrib separates Connemara from the rest of Ireland. Many people go to holiday in Connemara and are so busy getting there that they scarcely give a thought to the biggest lake in the State. But Corrib deserves something more than a thought — perhaps a week but certainly a day to make the circuit.*

# CORRIB COUNTRY

The journey from the city of **Galway** begins in the same way as a trip to Connemara, by following the road for **Clifden**. From a green hillside north of the city you get glimpses over or through a wall to the right of the lower part of the lake, where it narrows to form the smallest big river of Ireland: all eight miles of it. There is a distant view across the lake to a level plain with just one small hill to break the horizon.

At **Moycullen** you may stop and visit an emporium where they deal in Connemara marble, a beautiful stone in many shades of grey and green, polished and made by local craftsmen into anything from small jewels to large table tops. Moycullen is also where you turn right at the crossroads to take a more than ordinarily tortuous track towards the lake. Follow the main road, such as it is, between little fields bordered with stone walls or hedges of hawthorn. Here you can see farming methods which have disappeared from richer parts of the country fifty years and more ago: corn stooks and little haystacks.

About six miles from Moycullen comes a crossroads with an enticing signpost to **Knockferry,** a tiny harbour by the lake, and a lovely spot for a picnic or even a meal in the restaurant nearby. The route continues through **Coolnamuck,** along by hazel bushes which now and again part to give a view of the sparkling blue of the lake. Turn left at a T-junction to regain the main road for Clifden, but do not fail to turn off about a mile farther on where a big signboard shows the way to **Aughnanure Castle.**

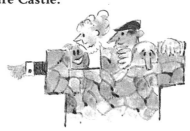

It is a great tower house, seething with history which you may read about in a leaflet costing fifty pence. But the history palls to insignificance beside the charm of the place. Walk to the castle beside a dark and silent stream which flows gently to Lough Corrib. Pass the time of day with a white goat who likes to have her head scratched, cross the river by a natural arch where the water has tunnelled through the limestone and meet the custodian's beautiful sheep dogs.

Then wander around the walls and inspect the turrets and finally enter the castle which, in the course of many years of careful restoration work, has had its woodwork replaced with modern replicas hewn from oak trees. Finally make your way to the parapets for a fabulous view over the lake and away to the hills of Connemara.

Back on the Clifden road, you meet the busy village of **Oughterard,** full of shops and good things to buy and well supplied with hotels. A wonderful diversion from the village leads along a road to nowhere but which keeps close to the lake and ends in sight of the dark and mysterious **Hill of Doon.**

From here you must go all the way back to Oughterard, taking the road through the village in the direction of **Maam Cross** and maybe stopping just once more at the tiny riverside park where you can sit under linden trees, watch the trout rising in the clear stream and gaze into a cavern across the water.

Then the road rises, turns a corner and suddenly brings you into **Connemara.** The change in the landscape is dramatic. Green fields, stone walls and an abundance of homesteads are replaced by wild moorland with bog, mountains and one small lake after another. The lakelets are a home for white water lilies, flowers which would grace any garden but are treasures in the lonely wilderness.

**Maam Cross** offers a choice of three roads, each one heading off into incomparably beautiful countryside. The right turn is the one to continue the circuit of Lough Corrib. It leads past a sad and

abandoned railroad station, untenanted by trains for more than sixty years, and into the mountains, descending by a twisting road to the bridge and shop. These constitute the port of Maam, in days gone by the terminus of a river boat which steamed all the way from Galway.

**Lough Corrib** comes into view again a little farther on, a remote arm of the lake with an island and a fairytale castle, **Castlekirke,** which has stood there for seven hundred years. It conjures visions of maidens held in durance vile, even if the name and legends associated with it refer mainly to an enchanted hen.

The road goes over the hill and descends again to run close to the lake shore for most of the way to the village of **Cong.** A little way before the village you cross a stone bridge which spans a very remarkable excavation. It looks as if it should be a river but is in fact a might-have-been canal. The engineers who planned it had forgotten that the limestone rock in the region has so many fissures and swallow-holes that the water from time to time takes a downward rather than a horizontal path, leaving the poor canal dry.

Cong was the site of a great abbey whose remains you may visit and much of whose sculptured stone was the work of a 19th century craftsman rather than of the monks of old. But visit it just the same and walk through the abbey to the silent wood of spreading yew trees beside the river and the little stone house where the monks caught their fish.

**Cong,** like Oughterard, has many places to stay, including **Ashford Castle,** begun in 1228 but enlarged and modern-

ised as a Guinness family mansion in the 19th century. The greater part of the demesne is public property and a drive through the grounds down to the lake is delightful.

After Cong the road stays away from the lake for much of the way back to **Galway.** Signposts from time to time show the way down to quays or piers, any one of them a pleasant diversion. Don't, however, forget to stay on the main road just north of **Headford** to see the splendid ruins of the great Franciscan friary of **Ross Errilly.**

The best of the diversions is indicated by an almost invisible signpost five miles south of Headford. It is **Annaghdown,** with yet one more ruined monastery. Search this one carefully for charming details in the sculptured masonry. Find in particular a small beast with enormous eyes engaged throughout the centuries in munching the foliage of the decorations.

One last diversion is the very well hidden village of **Menlough.** Turn right at the second crossroads after the broad Clare River. It is back once more to the winding, climbing roads of the southern part of the lake. Menlough is the only Irish-speaking community east of Lough Corrib and has retained the atmosphere of an old-world settlement, in spite of the building of many modern homes. The road leads down past tiny thatched cottages to a little riverside harbour. There the villagers have recently erected a memorial to a departed rowing team, who twice won the all-Ireland championship. Menlough is a mile from the busy suburbs of Galway and rejoices in an atmosphere a thousand miles from anywhere. •

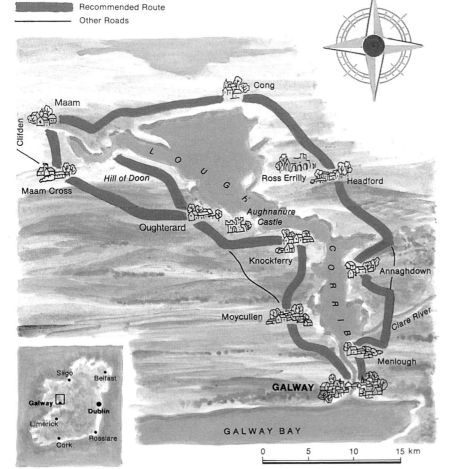

Recommended Route
Other Roads

| Distances | km | miles |
|---|---|---|
| Galway – Aughnanure | 34 | 21 |
| Aughnanure – Oughterard | 5 | 3 |
| Oughterard – Maam Cross | 19 | 12 |
| Maam Cross – Cong | 34 | 21 |
| Cong – Ross Errilly | 16 | 10 |
| Ross Errilly – Annaghdown | 19 | 12 |
| Annaghdown – Menlough | 19 | 12 |
| Menlough – Galway | 3 | 2 |
| Round trip | 149 | 93 |

## 10 TO THE MOUTH OF THE MOY

**Highlights:** Busy town of *Ballina* with salmon to fish for — or just to watch traditional fishing. *Rosserk friary*, peaceful ruins of an old monastery down by th shore. Bigger monastery at *Moyne*. *Killala* harbour and cathedral town. *Rathfran* yet one more abbey, and nearby a court cairn, stone age grave more than five thousand years old. *Breastagh* ogham stone and many other relics of bronze ag and iron age. *Rathlackan* close to site of historic landing of French troops in 1798 *Downpatrick Head* gentle grassy hill ending in magnificent sea cliffs. Beautiful lake drive around *Lough Conn*.

*The employment contract of the apprentices in the town of Ballina stipulated that they were not to be fed on salmon more than three times a week. It's a good story, in no way weakened by the fact that nobody can ever find a copy of the contract and that the same tale is told in a great many towns in Europe and North America.*

# to the Mouth of the MOY

If you visit **Ballina** in July you can linger by the **River Moy** where those fabulous salmon really are caught. At low tide the boats go to work, paying out a long net behind them as they cross the river, circling back to the shore and hauling in the net, sometimes with nothing in it, sometimes with silvery salmon by the dozen. A little way upstream, for a reasonable fee, you may enjoy some of the finest rod fishing for salmon in the world.

Salmon were immensely important in the past. Less than a couple of hundred years ago, good food always became scarce in winter. The only way of preserving meat and fish was the none-too-appetizing use of salt. But salmon swim up rivers like the Moy at midwinter and so the people who lived by its banks expected to be well fed and prosperous. This may explain why the region enjoyed a period of affluence in the Stone Age and for thousands of years thereafter.

A journey down the Moy from **Ballina** therefore brings you nowadays through a community of scattered farms punctuated every few miles by some relic of more affluent days. The route begins by taking the road to **Killala.** At a crossroads, 6 km north of Ballina, the first of a series of signposts shows the way to **Rosserk Abbey,** leading through increasingly narrow lanes towards the riverside: lanes so seldom used that grass grows along the middle line.

The final approach is down the narrowest of them, past a lonely farmstead and round a corner. Suddenly and dramatically, the grey walls of the Abbey and the blue water of the Moy appear before you. At high tide, the waters come close to the buildings. When the tide falls, it reveals sand banks, where curlews stride about, stabbing the ground with their long curved bills in search of deeply-buried worms.

**Rosserk** was a friary, built in the 15t century for the Franciscan monks. For th experts, it has many interesting feature beautiful stone tracery in the window delightful little carvings of angels and of round tower like the one not far away a **Killala.** But any visitor, expert o architecture or not, can have a wonderfu time there, climbing innumerable ston staircases and wandering through th monastic buildings.

Follow the lane back and turn right a the T-junction to drive over the green hill and enjoy a wonderful view of the Mo and its islands, fringed with white sand There is another friary, **Moyne Abbey,** km to the north of Rosserk. It is bigger an was a very important ecclesiastical centr in the 15th and 16th centuries. But th present day approach to the ruins is by muddy track through a field of cows – s you might succumb to the temptation o just admiring it from the roadside. But i you are brave, or wear wellies, you ca explore Moyne and climb to the top of it tower.

**Killala,** the next town, has a wall and many neat old houses. The rather smal cathedral has a fine spire and beside it i the round tower, a thousand years old, the relic of a monastery founded by St. Patrick himself five hundred years before the tower was built. Killala has a large harbour, but the sea is shallow and the fishing boats all tie up at the far end of the breakwater.

The road goes westwards from Killala, crossing the head of a long, winding creek by an eleven-eyed bridge. There a signpost points the way to **Breastagh Ogham Stone,** one of a fantastic array of prehistoric stone things on the headland to the north and west. There are more than twenty of them. On the way to the ogham stone you pass one more medieval monastery, down on the right. It is the Dominican friary of **Rathfran,** very much older than the Franciscan foundations to the south. Begun in 1274, it was rebuilt and enlarged over and over again for the next three hundred years.

At the crossroads, the most convenient of the stone-age tombs can be visited. Four pairs of large boulders form its sides. Like the majority of its companions on the headland, it is a court-tomb, so called because a semicircular open space or "court" was marked out by stones in front of the rectangular burial chamber. These tombs are the oldest of all the stone-age burials to be found in Ireland, going back as far as five thousand years.

A little way to the north of the crossroads, on the road for **Lackan Bay,** a signpost shows where to climb over the fence to see the ogham stone. It is a tall

pillar, with angular edges, well polished in its lower parts by generations of cows who like to scratch themselves on it, regardless of its profound historical significance.

Ogham was the earliest kind of writing used in Ireland, developed about 300 AD, long before the Christians introduced the Roman script. It is formed of little groups of straight lines: some at right angles, some sloping, above or below or through the line made by the angle of the stone. This one commemorates the son of Corrbri, the son of Amloitt. But the cows have worn away his own name. While the ogham belongs to the Iron Age, the stone itself may very well be a menhir, erected centuries earlier by Bronze Age people.

After Breastagh, the road goes through **Rathlackan,** passing by Lackan Bay. On

the side of the road there is a memorial to the successful landing of French Republican troops who came to the aid of the Irish freedom movement of 1798.

**Downpatrick Head** is a place of gentle, grassy slopes leading to tremendous cliffs. A lovely road runs around it to the village of Ballycastle. There you should be tempted to rent a well-appointed cottage and stay for a week or more to explore one of the least known and most dramatic parts of Ireland. But if you must hurry back take the road south to Crossmolina, perhaps making one more diversion to drive beneath the noble mountain **Nephin** and the incomparable **Lough Conn.** ●

| Distances | km | miles |
| --- | --- | --- |
| Ballina – Rosserk | 11 | 7 |
| Rosserk – Killala | 8 | 6 |
| Killala – Breastagh | 7 | 4 |
| Breastagh – Ballycastle | 19 | 12 |
| Ballycastle – Crossmolina | 21 | 13 |
| Crossmolina – Ballina | 12 | 7 |
| Round trip | 78 | 49 |
| Crossmolina – Ballina by Lough Conn circuit | 37 | 23 |

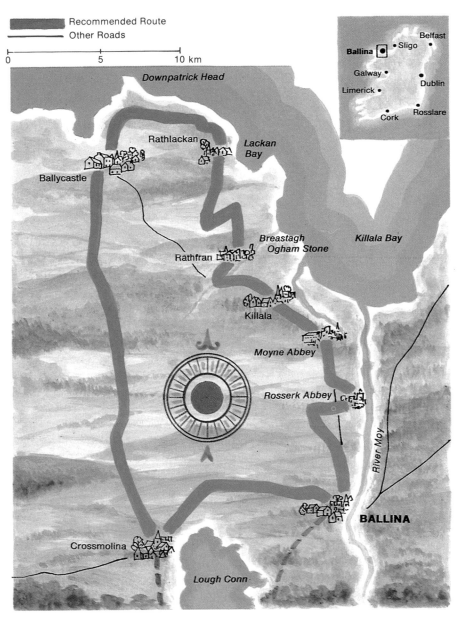

Recommended Route
Other Roads

0          5          10 km

*Highlights:* Fabulous salmon-fishing metropolis of *Ballina. Ballinglen* valley with ruined castle and iron age fort. Stone age tombs at *Ballyglass.* Some of Ireland's finest sea cliffs round about Downpatrick Head. Stone age farms and 20th century interpretive centre of *Ceide Fields.* Exotic crops at *Glenamoy.* Loneliest bog in Ireland in *Bangor Erris.* Shellfish farms at *Curraun* and endless views of magnificent mountains, lakes and seaside all the way.

*The northwest of County Mayo is the most ruggedly beautiful region of Ireland. It is the place to go when you want to immerse yourself in the grandeur of mountains and sea cliffs, a place which seems to be poor and inhospitable and yet where you can find farmers whose ancestors have tilled the land for five thousand years. And above all it is a region almost unknown, the last great tract of Ireland awaiting discovery by tourists.*

# Mountains of Mayo

The journey begins in **Ballina,** a busy town on the **River Moy** where there are so many salmon that thousands of people come to fish for them. This means that there are good hotels and guest houses in plenty. Signposts for **Belmullet** show the way out of Ballina through a gently rolling land of green pasture. What is particularly striking about the country here is the scarcity of trees. Even the hawthorns which form the hedges have a ragged look about them.

Five miles out from Ballina you cross a river, flowing southwards and a mile farther on you meet it again, flowing in the opposite direction. This is the **Deel River** which comes westwards from the mountains, then heads towards the sea and changes its mind to come back again to **Lough Conn,** the big beautiful lake which lies a little to the south of **Crossmolina.** But it is a very popular spot and therefore not on our itinerary.

So at **Crossmolina** you take the right turn for **Ballycastle** and drive through the same rolling green land for about nine miles to the valley of the **Ballinglen River.** For two thousand years, and probably more, it was a place of considerable importance. The good pasture meant wealth, and down on the left on a knoll in the floor of the valley there stands an ivy-covered ruin of a castle, a tower house dating to the 15th century. A mile farther on, surrounded by trees, a church, windowless and roofless, fights a losing battle against the elements. And, finally, on the left opposite a new bungalow before you enter the village, there is a 'ring fort', a circular mound protected by two banks with a ditch in between. Like the castle, it was a fortified dwelling but a great deal older, going back to the Iron Age, two thousand years ago.

The houses of the neat village of **Ballycastle** cling to the hillside and you turn left on the main road. The next left turn, just after the road downhill goes sharply to the right, takes you across the river by one of three beautiful stone bridges and up the hill to a crossroads in the hamlet of **Ballyglass.** The route turns right, but you may stop and walk up the hill to look at the very overgrown remains of a 'court tomb'. It consists of a little circle of stones covered with moss and lichen and it has a companion 50 yards to the north. Court cairns are Stone Age monuments, as much as five thousand years old. The foundations of a wooden house were found beside the northern one.

After **Ballyglass,** the road keeps close to the coast. There is little traffic, so little that any driver you meet will give you a cheerful wave of the hand. Surprisingly, there is a restaurant and guest house by the roadside. After this, the road takes a bend to go up a valley and the country changes completely: the green pasture is replaced by brown moorland where peat bog has formed a blanket over the entire landscape.

Then you come to a place where the road barely manages to keep out of the sea and there is a steel barrier to keep wayward cars in safety. It is a place to stop and admire the colourful cliffs, like a slice of cake with layers of black, grey, brown and purple. Away in the distance is **Downpatrick Head** with a great detached rock stack at its point. Amazingly, there were two houses on the stack in times gone by.

A little way on there is the first of two archaeological sites where Stone Age boundary walls have been found at the base of the blanket bog. It is signposted

'Ceide fields' on the left. Archaeologists have dug little pits in the peat to reach down to the foundations of the walls. The stones, protected by the acid soil for millennia, are sparkling bright and fresh. Their presence shows that, four or five thousand years ago, farmers had developed a system of land enclosures very much the same as those still in use. But they had a problem: the climate became more rainy and peat bog grew up over many of their fields.

The Ceide Fields have become one of the most celebrated archaeological sites in Ireland. You may enjoy the atmosphere as you walk amongst the fields or imbibe knowledge about them in great comfort within the interpretive centre which was opened in 1992.

Nowadays the peat has stopped growing and the farms are moving back again where it has been cut away. The marvellous thing about the landscape here is that, if one of the Stone Age people came to look at it today, he would see very little change. Perhaps a promontory or two have fallen into the sea since his time. The

telephone lines would certainly puzzle him and he would be amazed to see how much bigger the sheep are nowadays.

The moorland gives way to pasture once more and you come to the village of **Belderg** or **Belderrig.** A signpost leads to the second of the Stone Age sites, bringing you down by a lovely trout stream and up a short way into the hills. The excavated remains include the stone foundations of a circular house. New wooden poles have been arranged inside to show where the original timbers supporting the roof were placed.

After **Belderg** the road winds its way through alternating bog and pasture, past **Glenamoy** where New Zealand flax and rhododendrons and shelter belts of pine are mementoes of an agricultural research station. There is a very tempting road to

the right at Glenamoy, with a signpost pointing to about five lonely settlements. These are spread out along the coast, each associated with a tiny harbour whence the farmer-fishermen set out for salmon, lobster and mackerel. The roads are narrow and winding and bumpy and each one leads to loneliness and savage scenery.

After **Glenamoy** the route passes close to the lonely shore of **Carrowmore Lake** and then to **Bangor Erris,** where the peat is being extracted on the grand scale. Miles and miles of polythene sheeting keep it dry. On all sides there are mountains: the **Nephinbegs** to the left and, away on the right, the great hills and cliffs of **Achill Island. Achill** has a character all of its own, abounding in mountains and cliffs longing to be climbed, lakes to fish in and a heavenly strand. It is a way of life in itself, inhabited largely by people who, after one holiday there, spend their lives coming back again, never wanting to go anywhere else.

You pass the long, winding sea inlet of **Curraun** where salmon and mussels are farmed and then go amongst rhododendrons in a rocky gap to come suddenly into the totally different world of **Clew Bay.** In an instant the bogs disappear, there are green hills and trees and hotels and supermarkets.

A good road leads along the north side of the bay, with the Nephinbegs to the left and the holy mountain of **Croagh Patrick** to the right. There are castles and abbeys

and much else to look at on the way, but they can wait for another day. You could end the journey at **Mulrany** and mull over the possibilities of a trip to Achill Island or around Clew Bay or even back through more mountains to **Ballina.**

| Distance | miles | km |
| --- | --- | --- |
| Ballina – Ballycastle | 20 | 32 |
| Ballycastle – Belderg | 9 | 14 |
| Belderg – Bangor Erris | 16 | 26 |
| Bangor Erris – Mulrany | 19 | 31 |
| Mulrany – Newport | 11 | 18 |
| Newport – Ballina | 29 | 47 |
| Round trip | 104 | 168 |

A comfortable day trip from Ballina. ●

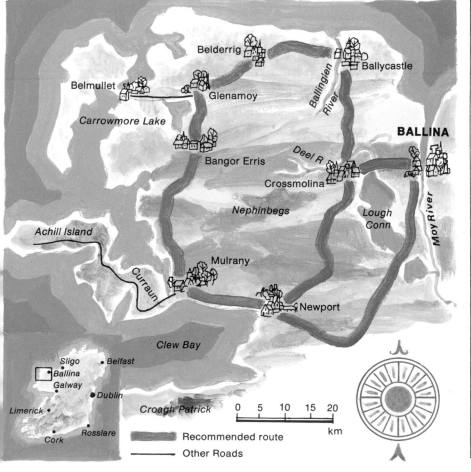

Belderrig

Ballycastle

Ballingien River

Belmullet

Glenamoy

Carrowmore Lake

BALLINA

Deel R.

Bangor Erris

Crossmolina

Nephinbegs

Lough Conn

Moy River

Achill Island

Mulrany

Curraun

Newport

Clew Bay

Sligo • Belfast
Ballina
Galway
• Dublin
Limerick •
Rosslare
Cork

Croagh Patrick

0  5  10  15  20
km

Recommended route
Other Roads

## 12 SLIGO TO GALWAY

*Highlights:* Lakeside woodland at *Ballygawley. Lough Nasool* with ancient pagan legendary associations. Stone age grave at *Heapstown.* Particularly beautiful lakes *Arrow* and *Key.* Birthplace of Percy French near *Boyle.* Iron age ring fort at *Tulsk.* Huge 13th century ruined castle at *Ballintober.* Cathedral town of *Tuam* with old and new cathedrals, a celtic cross and a watermill museum. Franciscan friary of *Claregalway.*

*On the highway a few miles to the south of Sligo there are two byways on the left. The signposts are festooned with names which come tumbling out of the poems of W. B. Yeats. If you take the road which leads to Dooney Rock and the Lake Isle of Innisfree you will be led to such an enchanting part of Ireland that you run the risk of forgetting the point of this journey which is to reach the city of Galway. That is why you must follow instead the sign which says 'Drumshanbo'.*

# Sligo to Galway

It leads you quickly out of the suburbs and into **Union Wood** which is so close to **Sligo** that you should not really think of stopping there for a picnic. But there is a convenient parking place beside a particularly beautiful stretch of water, **Ballygawley Lake.** It lies amongst the hills, completely surrounded by forest: birch and

spruces and pines, giving an impression of a little piece of Finland that got carried away by mistake.

Nine miles southeast of Ballygawley Lake a road runs off to the right between a shop and a large yellow-painted house. It takes you to two lakes which snuggle in amongst the green, rolling hills. First you go along the side of the kidney-shaped **Lough Bo** — the cow's lake. After a right turn the road rises and crosses a ridge to give a view down on the mystical **Lough Nasool,** the lake of the eye. The eye was the eye of Balor,

king of the Fomor which had to be kept covered up because, we are told, one look really could kill. Fortunately, the water has softened its glance and nothing disturbs the surface of the lake but the ripples made by a pair of swans. Once every hundred years the lake dries up and perhaps Balor stalks once more the kingdom which he lost so long ago. The last occasion was in 1931 so you are likely to be safe from his evil attentions for some time to come.

At the bottom of the next hill you turn left at the very appropriately named crossroads of **Heapstown.** The heap is of grey lumps of limestone, surrounded by a kerb of carefully selected boulders. Nearly as high as the gnarled trees that surround it, the heap is believed to be a passage grave — though nobody has ever found the passage and chamber which would lie within. From Heapstown you have a clear view of the flat-

topped **Bricklieve Mountains** where there is a great cemetery with tombs of the same kind and age — about four thousand years.

The road continues to run towards the southeast and brings you past two of Ireland's most beautiful lakes: **Arrow and Key.** You stay close to the edge of **Lough Arrow** and then climb over the ridge which separates the two lakes. There are many tempting stopping places by their shores but, if you are serious about getting to Galway, you must proceed through the town of **Boyle** in the direction of **Roscommon.**

This is sheep country, a land of green fields as far as the eye can see — and that is very far because the hills are all small and gentle ones. Occasionally, by way of diversion, the road takes you through a patch of moorland with peat bog and heather, but the green pasture with its grey stone walls and white sheep quickly reasserts itself.

Twelve miles down the road from **Boyle** a signpost points the way to the Birthplace of Percy French. A diversion of a mile or two along narrow roads takes you to a little memorial which stands on the site of his old homestead. A limestone figure of the immortal Inspector of Drains, creator of Phil the

Fluther and discoverer of the Mountains of Mourne gazes contentedly over the gentle land around.

The road wanders on passing through a succession of villages which basically are crossroads where people over the years built houses and set up shops. But most of them also have claims to very respectable antiquity and are provided with earthworks, castles and medieval churches to prove it. On the right in **Tulsk** you find an Iron Age ring fort: a circular grassy mound surrounded by a ditch: the mound would have been higher and the ditch deeper in days gone by.

**Ballintober** has the finest of the ruins in the region, visible from far away, two great ivy-covered towers at the corners of an impregnable enclosure of stone. It was built by the royal family of O'Conors in or about 1300, fought over, taken and rebuilt for more than three hundred years, taken by the Cromwellians and subsequently restored and lived in for another two centuries. It

fairly seethes with history and atmosphere. The farther off of the two towers, in spite of its sorry state of delapidation, holds memories of better times. Stand in its great hall and look upwards to the enormous stone fireplace which still seems to radiate warmth and well-being.

There is another castle and the remnants of a monastery at **Dunmore** but the next really important stopping place is the busy market town of **Tuam.**

It has been a busy market town for at least seven hundred years and seven hundred years before that began its

importance as a monastic centre. Time is of little consequence in Tuam, a point made by the town clock whose faces fail to agree with one another. Park your car and take a leisurely walk around, going to see the old water mill and its museum — saved from ruin by an inspired group of local students in 1970. Then visit St. Jarlath's Cemetery where you can follow the historical trail marked out by stone inscriptions or sit in the shade of a community of Irish yews, dark green and stately trees. For good measure there are two cathedrals as well, one of them with a large and well-preserved romanesque chancel.

The final part of the journey to Galway follows a highway — the byways in this region are too small and too many to be able to follow without getting thoroughly lost. And anyway it is essential to visit the ruins of the great Franciscan friary of **Claregalway** which the byways would miss. It stands boldly out in the plain, with a distant backdrop of the mountains of **Connemara.** Friars take a personal vow of poverty but, happily for people who like old buildings, this did not prevent them from

accepting lavish sponsorship and it seems that the great chieftains of east Galway vied with each other to build bigger and better homes for the friars. Most of the delicately sculptured stonework has been removed — but there is just enough left to allow you to imagine how it must all have looked in the great days of the 15th century.

From **Claregalway** a short journey brings you to a less dignified, if more familiar, world of shopping centres and traffic. The journey can be made comfortably in a day. ●

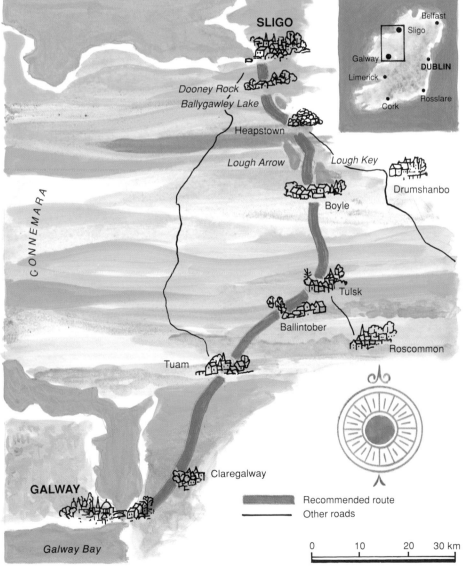

| Distances | km | miles |
|---|---|---|
| Sligo to Lough Nasool | 38 | 24 |
| Lough Nasool to Boyle | 37 | 23 |
| Boyle to Ballintober | 48 | 30 |
| Ballintober – Tuam | 34 | 21 |
| Tuam – Claregalway | 35 | 22 |
| Claregalway – Galway | 11 | 7 |
| | — | — |
| | 203 | 127 |

*Highlights:* Old world harbour with excellent restaurants and stately home to visit at *Westport*. Fishing harbour with traditional curraghs at *Murrisk*. Sacred mountain of *Croagh Patrick*. Primeval oakwood at *Old Head*. Ferry to *Clare Island* from *Roonagh Quay*. Unique 'marigold' cross in *Killeen Churchyard*. Clapper bridge of *Bunlahinch*. Remote seaside coves and craft shops around *Killadoon*. Stone-age wedge tomb by the roadside at *Lough Nahaltora* and stumps of prehistoric forest on lakeshore nearby. Mountain passes and lakes, the great sea inlet of *Killary Harbour* and wonderful waterfall at *Aasleagh*.

*Tradition tells that, somewhere amongst the mists of Mweelrea, there is a village which the tax-collectors have never discovered. Should you find it, don't tell anybody. Even if you, too, fail, you will at least be rewarded by the spectacle of some of the most magnificent and least known of the scenery of Ireland.*

# To the west of WESTPORT

The journey begins and ends in the very delightful town of Westport. From its tree-lined mall and adjoining stately home, signposts, first for **Clifden** and then for **Croagh Patrick** take you along the forbidding stone wall of the stately home, down to the old-world harbour.

The tall stone-built warehouses have little enough trade nowadays. But the harbour is a busy place with fishing boats and yachts and is quite exceptionally well-endowed with pubs and restaurants and craft shops. Over the hill from the harbour you descend to the sea shore and a view of the sheep-shaped islets of Clew Bay to the right.

To the left is the ridge of the sacred mountain Croagh Patrick but, before visiting it, you might be tempted to follow the signpost to **Murrisk Quay** which shelters lobster boats and curraghs, the traditional open boats which still compete happily with high-tech vessels.

**Croagh Patrick** is much more than a most spectacular peak. Christians respect it as a spot sanctified by St. Patrick who fasted there for forty days, thereby taking it over from the pagans who had worshipped there before him. On the last Sunday of July thousands of people gather from all over Ireland to climb the

mountain and stop to pray at certain points. Any other day of the year you can follow the path to the top and enjoy the solitude and a wonderful view of the west. In the car park at the foot of the mountain a Peace Tree grows. It was planted in International Peace Year, 1986.

From Croagh Patrick the road runs westwards toward **Louisburgh,** with a possible diversion to **Old Head** where there is a friendly hotel just below an ancient oak wood. Oak woods like this covered much of Ireland in the past. The few survivors are very carefully protected nowadays. Old Head, like Murrisk, has a little harbour for fishing boats.

The next village is **Louisburgh** where you turn southwards to cross the Bunowen River and meet a signpost which tells you of the many splendours of Killadoon. If you have a day to spare you should try the long straight road to **Roonah Quay** where you will find a

ferry port with an enticing invitation to travel to **Clare Island** and dine on fresh lobster. The island, like a great wall in the sea, stands about five miles offshore.

Early in the century it was the site of an international scientific survey and makes a fair claim to be the most intensively studied bit of Ireland. In 1991 a follow-up survey was launched to find out how things had changed.

From Roonah Quay the only way is back along the road nearly as far as Louisburgh where you head southwards towards **Killadoon.** The road rises and falls gently, running sometimes through green fields and sometimes through peat bog where hand-won turf is still the main fuel for heating. A modern bridge crosses the **Carrowniskey River,** rushing over its bed of great boulders, after which you come to the church of **Killeen.** In the cemetery by the roadside stands a tall pillar inscribed more than a thousand years ago with a marigold design. Close to the cemetery a signpost points to **Cross Strand** and **Bunlahinch Clapper Bridge.** The strand is one of many long beaches of pure white sand. The Clapper Bridge is unique, a footpath across a ford in a small stream. It has thirty stone piers, each pair spanned by a 'clapper', a flat slab of stone. Like the marigold cross, nobody knows who made it or precisely when – but it has certainly been there for a very long time.

The way goes on through the community of **Killadoon** – the homesteads, hotels and craft shops are so scattered that it scarcely constitutes a village. As the road climbs over the shoulder of **Mweelrea** and down again, the houses grow fewer and the fields stonier, and the stones bigger

until the road ends in a lonely sheltered cove. As at Roonah Quay there is no choice but to retrace your steps to the nearest crossroads which are at Killeen.

There you turn right and then left at the signpost for **Leenane**. This takes you over the northern slopes of Mweelrea, above **Lough Nahaltora** to the most visitor-friendly of the prehistoric tombs of Ireland. Most of the megaliths require the conquest of mountain slopes, or at the very least the negotiation of stone walls and five-barred gates. But the Wedge-Tomb of Lough Nahaltora stands proudly on a green patch at a fork on the road. A box of stone, capped by an enormous slab, it has great – if sacrilegious – possibilities as a picnic table. The lake

shore down below is studded with tree stumps: the last remnants of a forest which stood there until it was overwhelmed by the growth of peat. The forest may still have been thriving when the grave was built some four thousand years ago.

The road rises over the shoulder between the **Sheeffry Hills** and **Mweelrea** and then descends majestically to the wonderful valley where **Doo Lough,** the Dark Lake lies. Your drive along the shores of the lake is by courtesy of the Congested Districts Board which had the road built in

1896 and put up a carved stone plaque to tell of their achievement.

**Doo Lough** flows into a river which broadens again to form the smaller **Fin Lough,** the Pale Lake. A little way down the hill there will some day be a shady grove of native trees. A little too small to be shady, yet, they were planted by the Ministers for the Environment of the countries of the European Community to celebrate Earth Day, 22nd of April, 1990.

There remains a great deal of Environment to be seen before you return to Westport. The road first goes down the sparkling **Bundorragha River** where the shell fish produce fine pearls. These pearl mussels are now so rare in Europe that they are strictly protected by law. The river meets the sea in **the Killary,** a wonderfully long and narrow inlet of the sea which ends abruptly at the beautiful waterfall of **Aasleagh** where they filmed 'The Field'.

A mile down the road a signpost for **Westport** shows the way up the valley of the **Erriff** in the shade of **Devil's Mother** and the steep-sided **Partry Mountains**. There is an idyllic picnic place in the valley, six miles from the Killary, where the road crosses the Erriff and another of the ancient oak woods makes a canopy over a sward of green grass, cropped like a lawn by the sheep.

Then the road continues to follow the Erriff for a while before going over one more hill and heading down to **Westport,** giving on the way a farewell view of the great, white cone of **Croagh Patrick.** ●

|  | km | miles |
|---|---|---|
| Westport – Murrisk | 9 | 6 |
| Murrisk – Roonah Quay | 15 | 9 |
| Roonah – End of road | 18 | 11 |
| End of road – Lough Nahaltora | 11 | 7 |
| Lough Nahaltora – Aasleagh | 15 | 9 |
| Aasleagh – Westport | 22 | 14 |
| Total | 90 | 56 |

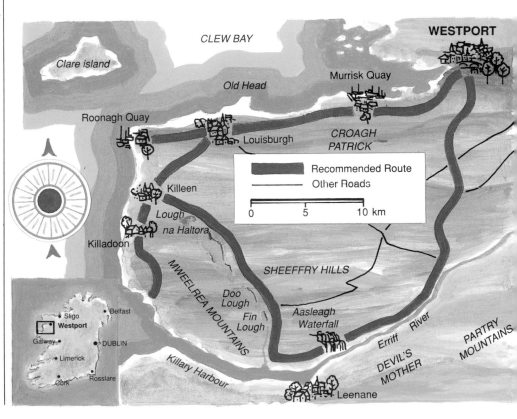

One of Ireland's finest bridges leads to the lighthouse on Mizen Head (Route 15).

## 14 THE LONG WAY TO KILLARNEY

*Highlights:* Traces of famous monastery of *Mungret.* Magnificent demesne of *Curraghchase* with endless acres of lovely parkland to wander in. *Askeaton* ancient friary on the river bank. *Foynes* on the Shannon with museum commemorating the harbour's great days as a transatlantic seaplane port. *Glin Castle* crafts and teas in stately surroundings. *Tarbert* with car ferry across the Shannon. *Beal* region of delightful little sandy coves. *Ballybunion* popular seaside place with magnificent strand, old castle, caves and cliffs. *Kerry Head* remote promontory with wonderful view of mountains and islands of Kerry.

*Such is the fame of Killarney that everybody wants to get there as quickly as possible. To do anything quickly in Ireland is, to say the least of it, thoroughly reprehensible. You will undoubtedly have a love affair with Killarney when you meet her, but there are attractions in a long and leisured courtship and a gentle and oblique approach has much to recommend it.*

# The long way to Killarney

Instead of taking the direct route, therefore, the plan is to go slowly along the coasts of Limerick and north Kerry, by roads which wander from one harbour to the next all the way to **Tralee**. There you go inland once more.

Before taking to the byways, it must be said that the main road from Limerick to Killarney is a lovely one. It goes through the exquisite village of **Adare** with its thatched houses and grey castles and churches and through many pleasant towns. You might be very wise to try it on the way back.

The journey begins by going through the stately streets of the city of **Limerick** and out into the suburbs until you turn right at a signpost for **Foynes**. At the edge of the suburbs the road passes through the ancient settlement of **Mungret**. The cement factory on the right with its tall chimneys draws your attention away from the plain stone wall on the left. It belongs to one of the three remaining churches of a great medieval monastery. The other two

are up a lane on the left and rather uninteresting — though I did meet a pheasant in the churchyard on my last visit. In its great days Mungret was a renowned seat of learning where fifteen hundred monks dwelt. Their piety and

scholarship were equalled only by their cunning in avoiding theological debate.

Sixteen kilometres farther on, a big signboard invites you to the wonderful demesne of **Curraghchase**. A long avenue winds its way for miles amongst trees, going downwards all the way, first through a thicket of young saplings and later past big conifers. Near the bottom of the hill, the woods give way suddenly to green, rolling parkland with a lake and swans in the valley. On the hilltop is the skeleton of a great, grey house.

Tragically destroyed by fire in 1941, it still stands defiantly, looking down over the magnificent oaks and cypresses planted a century and a half ago. It was the home in the 19th century of the poet Aubrey de Vere and a gathering place for

many of the greatest writers of the time. It remains, as it was in its great days, a place of peace and harmony, somewhere to spend hours walking beside the lake or over the hills amongst the trees.

Back on the main road, a much older foundation awaits you at **Askeaton**. It is the friary, founded for Franciscan monks by the Earl of Desmond, a little more than five hundred years ago. The monks have long since departed, but you can walk around the beautiful, vaulted cloister and feel their presence to this day.

The main road so far has kept a few miles away from the Shannon, though there are many tempting diversions down towards the water's edge. At **Foynes**, the whole scene changes when you go past the busy little seaport and round the steep hill with its forest to a road which stays close to the sea or, strictly speaking, to the estuary of the Shannon. Foynes has a very special place in aviation history as the base for transatlantic seaplanes, the forerunner of Shannon airport. Visit its museum.

The seaside road passes the gates of **Glin Castle** where you can buy craftwork and tea. The hills across the Shannon are in County Clare and you can take a ferry there from **Tarbert** to explore the wonderland of the **Burren** — provided you can spare a full day.

But if you are determined to make Killarney, continue through Tarbert, following first the signposts for **Ballybunion** then, at **Astee**, 7 km west of

**Ballylongford,** look out for a smaller signpost for **Beal,** where there are lovely little bathing beaches and a coast road. Tiny tracks lead down from the road to the coast where there are castles and cliffs. But the real centre of things is at Ballybunion. With its miles and miles of silver strand on the Atlantic coast, it is a very popular spot in summer. However, the strand is so long that it is possible to get away from everybody even at the peak of the season.

The road through the village takes you to the splendid remnants of a tall castle, overlooking the sea at the top of the cliffs, jet black cliffs stained in places with streaks of vivid ochre. Once upon a time they actually went on fire. In 1731 part of the cliffs to the north collapsed and became incredibly hot. The historian Charles Smith quoted a contemporary visitor: 'The mixture of burnt clay, ashes and calcined stones is worth observing but the heat is so great and the sulphurous stench so strong that there is no waiting to be over curious in making remarks.'

You walk through the entrance to the castle and out the other side since all that

remains of the building is the single, massively thick, wall. The view is magnificent, from **Loop Head** in the north, down to the mountains of the Dingle peninsula away to the south. Down below there are caves and up above, choughs fly by, jet black birds with blood-red bills which sail on the air currents by the cliffs. They are extremely rare, with one of their few surviving strongholds in Ireland.

From Ballybunion, the road goes southwards and then southwest to **Kerry Head,** a lovely promontory jutting out into the ocean. Rounding the head gives a marvellous view of **Slieve Mish** and **Brandon** and the other lordly mountains of Dingle. Closer by are the **Magharee Islands** and, all on its own out in the bay, the rock pinnacle called **Illaunabarnagh.**

**Ballyheigue,** on the south side of Kerry Head, is another popular seaside place. To the south you pass by **Akeragh Lough,** a small lake behind the sand dunes, famous among bird watchers who gather there every autumn to look for rare birds which have somehow gone astray and flown all the way across the Atlantic.

The land for the next few miles is strangely reminiscent of Holland, quite flat except where the sandhills rise on the coast. There are even small canals between the fields for drainage, but no windmills nowadays.

Then you come to **Ardfert,** a holy place for fourteen hundred years and more. It was founded by the great Saint Brendan who made an epic voyage over the ocean. Walk slowly and reverently around the ruins of the great 13th century cathedral and the even older little churches nearby. Rebuilding of them all took place again and again until the buildings were finally abandoned. There are traces of the work of many centuries, with lovely little sculptures and beautifully inscribed memorial tablets all over the place.

From Ardfert you head southwards, to the busy town of Tralee, immortalised in song and famous for its annual Rose of Tralee festival. One more hill remains to be climbed and then you slip down to the incomparable valley of Killarney.

from Tralee with Love

A comfortable day's journey allows an hour or two at each spot. Exploration of villages on the way or perhaps a cliff walk from Ballybunion to Beal would need an overnight break. ●

|  | km | miles |
|---|---|---|
| Limerick to Curraghchase | 22 | 14 |
| Curraghchase to Askeaton | 9 | 6 |
| Askeaton to Glin | 24 | 15 |
| Glin to Ballybunion | 32 | 20 |
| Ballybunion to Kerry Head | 28 | 17 |
| Kerry Head to Ardfert | 14 | 9 |
| Ardfert to Tralee | 8 | 5 |
| Tralee to Killarney | 29 | 18 |
|  | 166 | 104 |
| Killarney to Limerick direct | 111 | 69 |

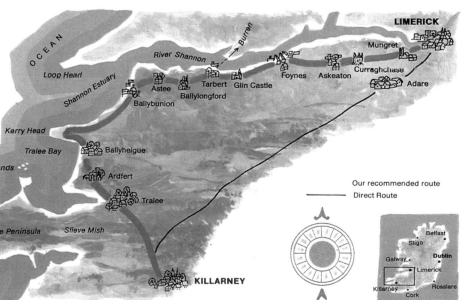

# SOUTH and SOUTHWEST

## 15 FROM CORK TO BANTRY AND BEYOND

*Highlights:* The famous castle of *Blarney* is a great deal more than a tourist trap: castle, great house, gardens and parkland. Historic town of *Macroom* with associations with William Penn. Man-made lake of *River Lee* near *Inchigeela. Lough Allua* natural lake of rare beauty. Ancient stone 'clapper' bridge at *Ballingeary.* Place of pilgrimage on lake island in *Gougane Barra*, home of the legendary but real 'Tailor and Ansty'. Mountain gorge in *Pass of Keimaneigh.* Seaside, scenery, old-world town and stately home all at *Bantry.* Extreme southwestern tip of Ireland at *Mizen Head* with cliff scenery and old lighthouse.

*West Cork is a place of contrasts, of green pastures so rich that great war lords built equally great castles to defend them, of miles and miles of rocky mountains where poor farmers struggled to survive. Rivers flow eastwards through the valleys and deep bays look out westwards to the ocean. Cork to Bantry is not a long journey: half a day if you hurry but enough to fill a week if you try to see everything.*

# From Cork to Bantry and beyond

The very idea of **Blarney,** the inanity of hanging upside down from the battlements to kiss a magic stone, is enough to induce any discerning person to give the region a wide berth. And that same person would be making the mistake of his erudite life. For the groves of Blarney, even when invaded by busloads of trippers, are a haven of peace in a busy world.

**Blarney** is the first village you meet on the byway from Cork to Bantry: set out on the Limerick road from Cork and look for a signpost to it before you pass the city limits. There is a visitor centre where they charge for admission and then you are free to wander over green lawns, shaded by immense lime trees, in the direction of the castle.

Standing above you on a precipice twenty feet high, it seems to reach to the clouds. Go inside and explore the labyrinth of passages and spiral stairs and poky rooms with tiny windows and be thankful that you are not forced to endure the discomforts of your affluent ancestors. And on the battlements you will need a strong will if you are not going to be cajoled by the custodian into kissing that stone.

After the castle, take a day to wander through the parkland to see the wonderful rock garden, to watch the beautiful fallow deer grazing in the park and then go to see the stately modern home, a mere hundred years old, with its treasures of art and furniture.

From Blarney follow the signposts for **Killarney** for a while, travelling through gently hilly country on a winding road sometimes open, sometimes shaded by tall trees. Near **Inniscarra** the first of two dams on the River Lee was built down in the valley. It is tantalisingly difficult to see the dam but, a couple of miles farther on, the County Council has made a parking place beside the waterworks and from that you have a pleasant view until the valley turns a corner and the lake disappears once more.

The byway goes through **Dripsey** where they spin wool and **Coachford** where you might divert to look for castles and forest parks and things or you might go on to the busy town of **Macroom.** It has a lovely market house, a large, sprawling castle and a small museum. In 1654 the castle was granted by Oliver Cromwell to Admiral Penn, father of William Penn, the father of Pennsylvania.

At Macroom take the main road back towards Cork for a little way and turn off at the signpost to **Inchigeela.** This road goes along the side of the upper of the two man-made lakes on the Lee, with a parking place beside an abandoned bridge. The

river at this point used to spread into a mass of small streams and the lake is studded now with tree stumps and tiny islands, bright in summer with yellow flowers. Farther upstream, a little piece of the Gearagh, as it was called, remains: an impenetrable jungle of willow and alder trees growing in the swamp.

Turn left in Inchigeela at Creedon's Hotel to take the south road along the exquisite **Lough Allua.** If you meet more than three cars in the course of the next six miles you have a right to begin to complain of traffic congestion. This road is known to practically nobody and you will probably have the entire lake to yourself. A Frenchman once said to a friend of mine there: 'But what is *wrong* with the water?' He simply couldn't believe that a place of such beauty could have so few visitors: not a boat, not even a single fisherman.

Leave the lake for a little to go over the hills by a zig-zag road and down into the valley again passing, opposite the village of **Ballingeary,** an ancient bridge built of 'clappers', big slabs of slatey rock. Nobody uses it to cross the river now because there is a beautiful four-arched bridge nearby. But the clappers are just the right height to sit on and dangle your legs above the water and that is what everybody does.

The road for **Bantry** passes both bridges and bears to the left. But there is a signpost to the right for **Gougane Barra** and that is a place that nobody should miss. A small blue house on the hillside was the dwelling of the legendary but very real Tailor who lived there nearly fifty years ago with his wife, Ansty. His life and his stories are among the most delightful in Irish literature.

Fifteen hundred years ago Saint Finbarr lived in a hermitage on the island of Gougane Barra Lake and it has been a place of pilgrimage ever since. The atmosphere that attracted the saint is still there: a placid lake surrounded by tall cliffs, a place of silence. The road goes on past the lake, heading into a narrow defile. Drive through the Forest Park there if you are in a hurry. But if you are sensible drive in and walk for miles beneath the green

trees and among the purple foxgloves, listening to the song of birds and the music of little waterfalls.

Then continue on the road for Bantry which climbs very soon afterwards through the magnificent **Pass of Keimaneigh,** a winding cleft in the mountains, studded with great walls of grey slatey rock, shrouded in green with ferns and hazel. It leads into more open land and so down the hill to meet the sea at **Ballylickey** which stands at the head of Bantry Bay.

Bantry itself is a lovely town with something of the air of a place that development forgot about two hundred years ago. There are excellent shops and inns and parking spaces, but the otherworldliness survives. Just outside the town is the entrance to Bantry House, a splendid

mansion of the early 19th century with gardens where you may wander at will, admiring the bay and the mountains — to say nothing of the neat rows of black and blue buoys where the most delectable mussels grow.

A modest payment admits you to the house which displays all that a stately home should: art treasures, furniture, tapestries. But somehow it does it with a

special charm. It is a family home and it feels like one: you are free to wander without the assistance of a guide. And then you can retire to the kitchen and enjoy tea and apple pie and buy lovely craft things. If you are especially lucky you will arrive on an evening when there is a concert.

And that should be enough for anybody. But I am greedy and on my last visit, set off for **Mizen Head.** You find it by driving past the harbour and following signposts to **Crookhaven** or **Goleen** first and then a 'Coast Road' and finally Mizen Head itself. It is the south-westerly extreme of Ireland, almost frightening in the magnificence of its cliffs. This is a place where the land of Europe is fighting a battle with the ocean — and losing. Inexorably the solid rock of the continent is being shattered and ground away and it looks wonderful.

| Distances | km | miles |
|---|---|---|
| Cork – Blarney | 10 | 6 |
| Blarney – Macroom | 37 | 23 |
| Macroom – Gougane Barra | 32 | 20 |
| Gougane Barra – Bantry | 24 | 15 |
| Bantry – Mizen Head | 48 | 30 |
| | 151 | 94 |

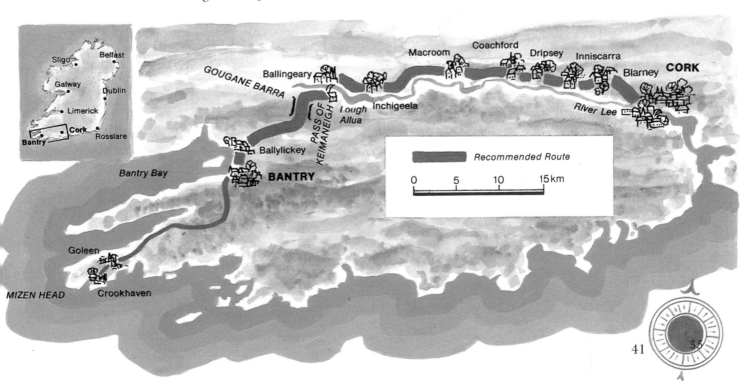

## 16 ROSSLARE HARBOUR TO CORK

*Highlights:* Fishing village with many thatched houses at *Kilmore Quay* and access to *Saltee* bird islands. Vanished seaport of *Bannow*, site of landing of Anglo-norman invaders. Ancient lighthouse and much more ancient fossiliferous rocks at *Hook Head*. Seafood and ferry at *Ballyhack*. Another fishing village with cliffs and birds and yachts at *Dunmore East*. Dolmen near *Tramore*. Dramatic *Dunhill Castle*. Cliff-top road with wonderful wild flowers to *Bunmahon* and remains of ancient mines. Irish-speaking community at *Ring*. Round tower at *Ardmore*.

*The south coast is a land of dreams, a place to wander through ever so slowly looking at wonderful things and remembering times long gone but vividly brought to life by castles, abbeys, thatched houses or even just by the names of places. And if the past means little to you, you may feast on the present: the wild flowers, the birds, the sea, and mile after mile of the most marvellous cliffs.*

# Rosslare Harbour to Cork

The journey begins at the ferry port of **Rosslare** where peaceful visitors make a landfall from Wales. Signposts tempt you away from the main road for Wexford to places like Lady's Island Lake but we will pass by that little corner of Ireland and head for **Kilmore Quay.**

The roads are narrow, and wind their way between hedges of gorse, passing **Bargy Castle,** still a family home five hundred years after it was built. That was where the rich lived. The poor inhabited

tiny thatched cabins and there are a few of them left, too. And, just outside the village of Kilmore Quay, a windmill tower stands. It is very easy to cast your eye over the flat country and imagine how it all looked a hundred years ago and more.

The village itself contains a great many thatched houses, most of them substantial two-storey buildings, the homes of generations of fishermen who catch

lobsters around the **Saltee Islands.** The islands, incidentally, are one of Ireland's best-known bird haunts and well worth a day-trip in summer, to see the tens of thousands of seabirds which nest there.

From **Kilmore Quay** follow the signposts, first to **Wellingtonbridge,** and then to **Bannow Island.** The road goes by the edge of a long, shallow inlet and below a ruined church on a hill. It was a big church and looks strangely out of place, even though surrounded by many tombs in a well-kept graveyard. A helpful plaque beside the gate explains it all. Here stood the town of Bannow, a thriving port until the swirling sands invaded the deep anchorage between the church and the island across the way. With no ships, the port faded into oblivion: first the people, then the houses disappeared and only the tombs remain. The island, too, has its place in history: this was the spot where, in 1169, rather aggressive visitors from Wales began their invasion of Ireland.

From **Bannow Island** the road goes around the Bay, passing an old mine chimney on the right, crossing the inlet at Wellingtonbridge and looking across to a lonely tower in a green field. Soon afterwards you meet the first of a series of signposts which take you around the **Ring of Hook.**

There is a **Tintern Abbey** down in the valley nearby, not the one in Wordsworth's great poem, but a "daughter house" founded in 1200. People still lived in it up to the 1960s, but now it is a pleasant ruin to wander around and worth taking the walk to see the beautiful stone bridge across the creek on the far side of the church.

From Tintern you go through **Fethard,** with Jinny O'Leary's fantastic garage and collection of brightly painted farm machinery of a not long past age. Then comes

**Hook Head** where the road to the lighthouse seems to go to the very end of Ireland. The Head is a long, low promontory, a place to visit in stormy weather to see the road covered with sea spray like

new-fallen snow; or to visit on a hot day to clamber over the cliffs and look at the fossils of three hundred million years ago. Above the cliff stands the massive tower of the lighthouse where a beacon has been lighting for eight hundred years.

There is not much choice at Hook Head but to drive northwards and so through a succession of delightful fishing villages until you come to **Ballyhack,** snuggling into the base of the cliffs. You might be lucky enough to miss the ferry there and succumb to the temptation to stop at the seafood restaurant nearby. Anyway, it is not a long wait and the ferry makes a lovely break in the journey as it brings you from Ballyhack to the equally delightful village of **Cheekpoint.**

If you are being sensible and taking this journey very slowly, there are many places to stay on the way but I can't help being most strongly tempted by **Dunmore East,** a very busy fishing harbour, the home of the boats which hunt the herring of the Celtic Sea. People keep yachts

there, too, and the harbour is surrounded by red cliffs inhabited by thousands of kittiwakes, exquisite little seagulls which snuggle together on the ledges.

The next large town is **Tramore,** which serves the thousands of people who come to enjoy the miles of beach and sand dunes. On the outskirts of the town a signpost beckons you to **Knockeen Dolmen,** one of many Stone Age monuments, perhaps five thousand years old. Knockeen is an easy one to find and needs only a short walk across a field to inspect it at close quarters.

After Tramore take a small diversion to look at **Dunhill Castle,** on its rock at the head of a valley and then prepare for the most beautiful cliff-top road in the world: miles of a journey amongst brilliant seaside flowers, pink, yellow and white. At **Bunmahon** there are fascinating — and highly dangerous — old mine workings.

The road continues to wind its way, climbing up and down the sides of small valleys, through **Dungarvan** and out to **Helvick,** through the community of **Ring** where Irish is still the daily language and then to **Ardmore,** the "great height" which must be our last stopping place. A graceful round tower stands above the walls of a once great cathedral, decorated by sculptured figures: some too worn to recognise, others almost as vivid as they were when carved a thousand years ago.

From Ardmore it is a short journey to **Youghal,** a town so stuffed with history that it needs a day to itself. And then you may go straight on to **Cork** — or you might go crooked and absorb even more coast road. But take care, you could easily end up never getting to Cork at all and it would be a pity to miss it.

| Distances | km | miles |
|---|---|---|
| Rosslare – Kilmore Quay | 21 | 13 |
| Kilmore Quay – Bannow Island | 22 | 14 |
| Bannow Island – Hook Head | 50 | 31 |
| Hook Head – Ballyhack | 13 | 8 |
| Passage East – Dunmore East | 13 | 8 |
| Dunmore East – Tramore | 19 | 12 |
| Tramore – Bunmahon | 32 | 20 |
| Bunmahon – Ardmore | 61 | 38 |
| Ardmore – Cork | 64 | 40 |
| | 295 | 184 |

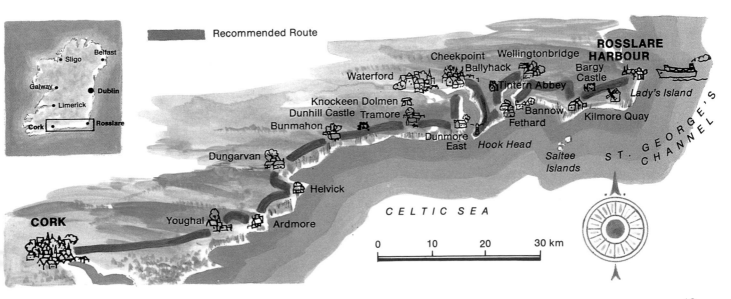

## 17 ONE DAY FOR DINGLE

**Highlights:** Mountain road with flowering hedges over *Slieve Mish*. Enticing strand and sand dunes at *Inch*. Seaside castle of *Minard*. Friendly dolphin to be visited at *Dingle*. Bronze age 'gallauns', huge boulders with traces of carving at *Milltown*. Beautiful bay of *Ventry Harbour*, site of great legendary battle. Ancient earthworks and remains of castle at *Dunbeg*. Stone-built 'beehive' huts at *Fahan* and view of Blasket and Skellig islands. Traditional village of *Dunquin*. Unique stone church of *Gallarus*. Another mountain road through the *Conor Pass*. Restored windmill near *Tralee*.

*To do Dingle in a day is sacrilege. But I did it. The just reward for my sins is remorse at having driven past so very many exciting things. Give the Dingle peninsula three days if you can — otherwise take the example of a plethora of poets and artists and spend all your holidays there. I offer this one-day trip as an enticement to greater things.*

# One day for Dingle

The journey begins in **Tralee** which you leave by the road for **Castlemaine.** At the crossroads, two miles south of the town, turn right to follow a very narrow and bumpy road to the next crossroads one mile farther on. There you turn left to begin a steep and tortuous ascent of the **Slieve Mish Mountains.**

It is a lovely lonely road: first of all running between tall hedges of hawthorn and shaded by ash trees. On the higher slopes hawthorn gives way to bracken and the first of the marvellous hedges of fuchsia. In August they are one of the great attractions of the whole peninsula, masses of crimson blossom.

Over the hill a parking place gives a view south and east to **Macgillycuddy's Reeks,** highest and most splendid of all Ireland's mountains. From the viewing point the road twists its way downhill again, and you take a right turn at the first crossroad, back again to hawthorn hedges in the lowland and on to a broader road along the edge of **Castlemaine Harbour.** On the right there are mountains all the way, while on the left the land slopes gently down to the seaside. In winter brent geese flock there, finding it rather warmer than their nesting places in arctic Canada. A gentle hill brings you across the

great sand barrier of **Inch,** the first of many fantastic beaches with miles and miles of clean, white sand. After running for some way above low red cliffs, the road turns inland up the Annascaul River towards the village of the same name. A little before you come to **Annascaul** a signpost shows the way to Minard Castle, standing above a small sheltered cove which it guarded until the Cromwellian soldiers blew it up — together with the garrison. The enormous beach pebbles, bigger than footballs, in front of the car park are a tribute to the fury of the ocean.

**Dingle** is a very busy place, completely taken over by a dolphin named Fungi. Time was when people went to Dingle to buy fish, to have seaside holidays and to learn Irish. Now they go to see the dolphin. On a summer's day boats go to the harbour mouth where Fungi meets them, swims from boat to boat and now and again obliges with

spectacular leaps. He is a totally wild and totally tame and friendly creature who likes to play with swimmers or just to look at less energetic visitors.

The road from Dingle to **Dunquin** is fairly littered with the leavings of several thousand years. You can begin to look for them by parking beside the white wall of the cemetery at **Milltown,** after passing the first signpost for **Slea Head Drive.** Across the road there is a gate from which you can see two enormous stones lying on the ground; a third stands close by in front of the next house. The bigger of the two on the ground is marked with little round hollows and some rather indistinct lines. After three thousand years of exposure it is not surprising that they are no longer easy to make out. The great stones are called 'gallauns' and belong to the Bronze Age when mining communities worked here.

The next bay is **Ventry Harbour,** where the white strand was the scene of an epic legendary battle in which the hero Fionn MacCool and his followers saved Ireland from invasion by no less a personage than the King of the World. (The invasion was not altogether unjustified: it was launched simply to aid

the king of France after Fionn had borrowed not only his wife, but his daughter as well).

Then you begin to climb the slopes of **Mount Eagle,** leading to **Slea Head.** The first stopping point is Dunbeg Fort which, according to a local handout, is 'notorious for its tranquility'. Four earthen banks protect a complex collection of stone buildings and there are underground passages as well, a lovely place to explore. It was still in use a thousand years ago.

Less than a mile up the road from Dunbeg is **Fahan** where you may park in front of a very old whitewashed farm house and pay a modest fee for admission to the incredible village just up the hill.

Within a compound stands a group of circular buildings. Some have been damaged but two remain in good order: beehive-shaped dwellings made with remarkable skill of stones without a trace of mortar. Who made them or precisely when remains a mystery but it is certain that they have withstood the gales of the Atlantic for one thousand years and maybe for two. From the village you also

get your first view of the **Blasket Islands** and, on a clear day, you can see the island of **Skellig Michael** where there are many more of the beehive huts.

The road goes around **Slea Head** and through the village of **Dunquin** which overlooks **Great Blasket Island,** now uninhabited and a National Park, but where an amazing community lived until quite recently. Not content with preserving the Irish language and their own way of life — they produced an astounding stream of world-class literature.

Antiquities, cliffs and beaches abound in the region — which is why you should take days rather than hours over it — but in the interests of the day trip we will ignore much. Go through **Bally-ferriter** and follow the signposts for **Gallarus,** the peak of perfection in rough-hewn stone. Quite a small building, its age is unknown but it is generally given a good thousand years or more. The age doesn't greatly matter when you look at the exquisite precision with which the stones were fitted together.

Continuing up and over the hill from Gallarus brings you back to **Dingle** where you find the left turn at the roundabout which takes you to the **Connor Pass.** The steep and narrow road leads to some of the most magnificent scenery in Ireland: the lonely lake-studded valley between the great mountains of **Brandon** and **Stradbally,** sweeping down to the sea and the distant islets of the **Maharees.**

At the bottom of the hill, the country is tame once again and we can take one more diversion, through the village of **Castlegregory** and along the extraordinary spit of sand for miles to the village of **Kilshannig.** Here there is a windswept churchyard, mostly filled by massive family vaults, but with a little old church and a very unusual carved cross. On the way back you can see on the left one more gallaun, a huge standing stone in a field testifying silently to some long-forgotten mystery.

Twenty more miles bring you back to Tralee, past a lovely windmill with a craft-centre and coffee and so to a very busy, very modern world again. •

| Distances | miles | km |
|---|---|---|
| Tralee – Inch | 20 | 32 |
| Inch – Dingle | 15 | 25 |
| Dingle – Dunquin | 13 | 21 |
| Dunquin – Gallarus | 8 | 13 |
| Gallarus – Connor Pass | 10 | 16 |
| Connor Pass – Kilshannig | 14 | 23 |
| Kilshannig – Tralee | 21 | 33 |
| Round trip | 101 | 163 |

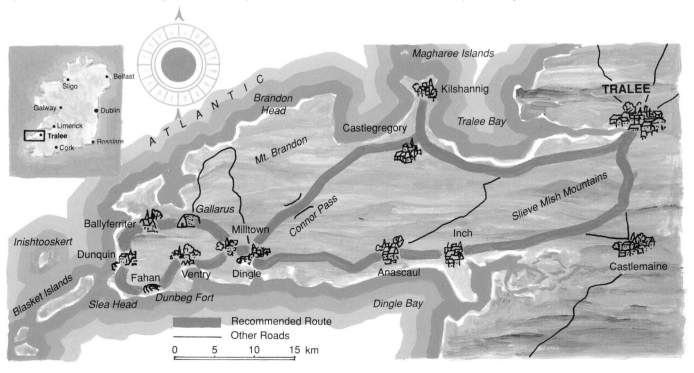

## 18 THE WEST OF MEATH

*Highlights:* Castle, church and echo of *NewtownTrim* and interesting memorial sculpture in the churchyard. *The River Boyne*, famous for its salmon for about five thousand years. *Trim Castle*, one of the finest in Ireland (see Route 35). Great peat bog beyond *Ballivor*. Restaurants at *Mullingar*. Peaceful lakeside stopping place at *Lough Owel*. Legendary dwelling of the Children of Lir at *Lough Derravaragh* and stained glass memorial to them in *Multyfarnham* abbey church. Stately mansion of *Tullynally Castle* open to visitors in summer. *Loughcrew* hilltop stone age cemetery.

*The counties of Meath and Westmeath once upon a time constituted one of the five kingdoms of Ireland. Their fertile land attracted settlers from the earliest times, and the region contains many of the greatest shrines of Irish heritage. This route avoids them all and looks at some lesser ones, those known only to the most discerning of wayfarers.*

# The West of Meath

There is something pleasing in the idea of a new town which consists entirely of buildings between five and seven hundred years old. Such is **Newtown Trim,** a place which would be famous were it not for the fact that the old town, called simply **Trim,** centres around a truly magnificent castle and an abundance of other antiquities.

The approach to **Newtown Trim** begins along the Navan road from Dublin, a route which is definitely not a byway, but which is so narrow and winding that it feels like one. You leave the Navan Road at a hamlet called Black Bull. There a large signboard shows the way to Trim, by a lovely road bounded by unkempt hedges

amongst green fields inhabited by peaceful cattle. It brings you to the green, grassy slopes of **the Boyne,** and so to the castles and churches of Newtown which provided temporal and spiritual protection to a crossing of the river.

Go across the narrow, five-arched stone bridge and enter the cemetery to admire many memorials to people of the 18th century and, the pride of the place, the boldly-carved recumbent effigy of a knight, Sir Luke Dillon, and his lady who died in 1586. After inspecting the ruins you may cross the river again and continue on the road to Trim. But stop beneath the great ash tree and walk to the gate opposite the ruins of the cathedral. Shout a few appropriately reverent words and wait for them to be returned by an incredibly clear echo.

It is easy to spend a long time in Trim before going on through **Ballivor** and **Killucan** and so to **Mullingar.** The road passes through a great tract of bog where the peat is being extracted by ponderous machines and then through a smaller bog, still uncut and bright with heather.

**Mullingar** is a busy town with a goodly variety of places to stop for a meal or a snack — unless you have already planned to enjoy a lakeside picnic. Our route follows the main road to Sligo for a mile and a half. In sight of the railway crossing, take the almost invisible turn to the left where a signpost says 'Sailing Club'. A very narrow road goes along by the edge of a stream and so to the shore of **Lough Owel,** a shore festooned with green-

painted rowing boats, but with little other sign of humanity: a lovely place where the silence is broken only by the song of birds and the lapping of the crystal clear water of the lake.

The Sligo road continues northwards, climbing above **Lough Owel** and then passing a smaller, reed-fringed lake. Turn right at an inn called The Covert to journey amongst green hills and look down over **Lough Derravaragh** before descending to the sleepy village of **Multyfarnham.**

It has a lovely church, with ancient stone memorial tablets and bright modern stained-glass windows. Four of these are dominated not by saints, but by swans. They commemorate the four children of Lir who were cursed for nine hundred years to take the form of swans. Three hundred of these years they spent on the nearby **Lough Derravaragh,** where you may see their descendants.

A signpost for **Coole** takes you past the end and the beginning of Derravaragh. It is a curious lake, six miles long, but with

inflowing and outflowing streams just a mile apart. People go fishing there, following a tradition of five and a half thousand years: important traces of Stone Age fishermen and hunters can still be found between the rivers.

The road leads around the northern part of Derravaragh to **Castlepollard,** a neat village with two churches whose tall, slender spires engage in dialogue across the fair green. A signpost shows the way to Tullynally Castle which opens its doors and its garden to visitors for just one month, from mid-July to mid-August. Tullynally began in the 19th century as quite a large family mansion and then proceeded to grow and grow, and become more and more of a fairytale castle. The Earls of Longford, who owned and embellished it, had a pleasing habit of not throwing things away so, besides castle and beautiful grounds, it is a treasure-house of old farm and kitchen equipment.

Back in Castlepollard, a signpost shows the way to **Oldcastle,** meandering through low limestone hills until, a little way short of Oldcastle, you come to the great mill of **Millbrook** where there is the first of several pointers to the **Loughcrew**

passage-grave cemetery. In Millbrook you pass a tiny 19th century school which has two doors, a memorial to the days when sexes were sexes, and boys and girls were so strictly segregated that they were required to use different entrances.

All good tourists know about the great passage-grave cemetery on **the Boyne** with the magnificent mausoleum of **Newgrange,** built five thousand years ago. The Loughcrew cemetery is less well-known and certainly less spectacular but, maybe because of this, having a special charm of its own. At Newgrange you have guides and postcards and a museum — at Loughcrew you have green hills, blue skies and sheep.

The custodian of the cairns lives in a farmhouse at the bottom of the hill and a notice at the gate announces that a key may be borrowed there. A steep, narrow road takes you over the hills to a car park from which you walk to the summit. The key will unlock the gate to Cairn T and afford faintly uncomfortable access along the passage into the central chamber. But crawl very slowly so that you can look at the abstract decorations which a sculptor, using only stone implements, carved more than two thousand years before the birth of Christ.

There are six smaller graves around Cairn T and dozens more on the neighbouring hilltops. You could spend a happy afternoon tramping the hillsides, looking at every one of them and gazing out over miles and miles of fertile plains,

studded with lakes and villages. The Neolithic farmers who built the tombs probably did likewise.

**Loughcrew** is the last stopping place on this route — you may go back to **Dublin** by way of **Kells** and **Navan** in an hour and a half. But you could equally well spend weeks or more looking at the wealth of ancient things that abound in the valley of **the Boyne.** One archaeologist has been at it for twenty-seven years and he is far from finishing.

The whole trip could be managed on a long summer's day. Better to take two or three days and stay in one of the many guesthouses which cater for fishermen or perhaps in some of the more affluent hotels where owners of race horses and cattle congregate.

| Distance | miles | km |
|---|---|---|
| Dublin – Newtown Trim | 27 | 43 |
| Newtown Trim – Mullingar | 27 | 43 |
| Mullingar – Lough Owel | 2.5 | 4 |
| Lough Owel – Multyfarnham | 6 | 9 |
| Multyfarnham – Castlepollard | 10 | 16 |
| Castlepollard – Tullynally | 1.5 | 2 |
| Tullynally – Loughcrew | 13 | 21 |
| Loughcrew – Kells | 12 | 19 |
| Kells – Dublin | 37 | 60 |
| Round trip | 136 | 217 |

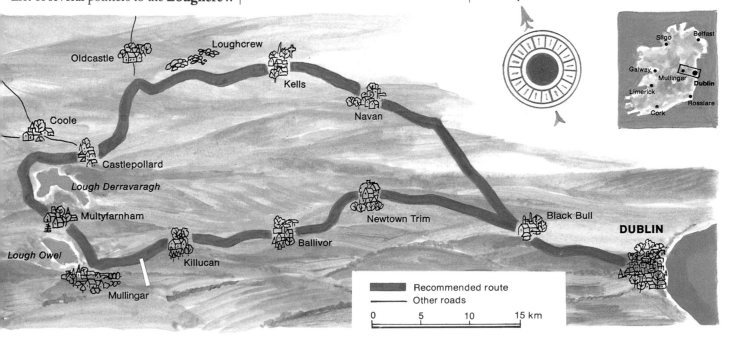

Recommended route
Other roads

0    5    10    15 km

**19** ON THE GREEN, GRASSY SLOPES OF THE BOYNE

*Highlights:* Wonderful collection of old farm and domestic implements and many other unusual artefacts at *Millmount Museum* in Drogheda. Peaceful backwater by the Boyne Canal at *Oldbridge* and signposted guide to the Battle of the Boyne. Possible diversion to *Mellifont Abbey* (scc Route 22). Woodland park at *Townley Hall*. World famous stone age cemetery at *Newgrange*. Birthplace of the poet *Francis Ledwidge*. Stately home of *Slane Castle*. Round tower of *Donaghmore*. Well preserved ruins of *Bective Abbey*. Sheelanagig at *Rosnaree* and small celtic cross at *Duleek*.

*Three hundred years ago a decisive battle was fought on the green, grassy slopes of the Boyne. But three centuries are a mere moment in the history of that beautiful river. The Boyne valley has been famous for nearly five thousand years: a legendary home of great gods, a proven site of almost incredible Stone Age technology — but above all a lovely, peaceful place to wander through with much more to look at than the great monuments.*

# On the green, grassy slopes of the BOYNE

Harry Fairclough was well over eighty when I met him and still riding his bicycle every day to the Millmount Museum. You find the museum by following a signpost to the old fortifications on the hill to the south of the Boyne in the city of **Drogheda**. It is a lovely place, largely Harry's own lifetime collection of ordinary things: from sewing machines to kitchen mangles and with a few extraordinary objects for good measure. Amongst the latter is a Boyne coracle, a tiny boat made and used by salmon fishermen still alive today, but to a design developed before the dawn of history.

The main road from **Dublin to Belfast** crosses the Boyne by a new bridge, but our route stays on the near bank and takes a narrow road up the hill and down again to run for a while along the side of the river. Here you meet a sad remnant of the **Boyne Canal:** sad because the lock is more than just derelict, it has actually been rendered totally unfit for passing boats by the building of a concrete bridge.

But a few miles farther on a very much more welcoming canal stretch waits to greet you. It begins at **Oldbridge,** the first crossing of the main river upstream of the many bridges of Drogheda. Here both canal and tow path have been cleaned up, the path spread with gravel and making a lovely walk with an ancient, swampy wood on one hand and a lush green watermeadow on the other. Just the place to stop for a morning picnic, stretch the car-cramped limbs and look for kingfishers.

Compared with many of the crossings of the Boyne, Oldbridge is positively modern, the creation of a 19th century iron-master. There is a curious outcrop of limestone rock beside the bridge on the left bank. On this you may just make out the remains of an obelisk erected to commemorate the Battle of the Boyne. It was destroyed long ago by persons unknown who felt the battle was unworthy of such commemoration. Signposts nearby show where the two protagonists: King James and King William had their respective encampments.

Another sign shows the way, not to a scene of hostility, but to a place of peace and contemplation, the old monastery of **Mellifont.** It is a very tempting diversion. Little enough remains of a splendid establishment: in the main the foundations of walls and the feet of great carved pillars. The joy of Mellifont lies in the silence of the green valley where no cars pass and few people visit. You may have it entirely to yourself of a summer's evening and listen to the music of the birds and the gentle river nearby.

Our main route goes along by the Boyne, stopping perhaps a little way upstream of Oldbridge where an entrance gate and a little lodge in the style of a Greek temple welcome you to **Townley Hall Wood.** It is a small woodland park

on the side of the valley with footpaths to bring you up the hill and look down over the river.

A short way farther on a signpost for **Dowth** shows the way to the great treasures of the **Bend of the Boyne.** On high ground above the river five thousand years ago a Stone Age community built three enormous burial mounds and countless lesser structures. First comes **Dowth,** then **Newgrange** and finally **Knowth.** There is an excellent museum and information centre at Newgrange, while at Knowth you may stand on a balcony and watch real live archaeologists at work. George Eogan, the leader of the project, started work there in 1962 and is a long way from finishing.

Some of the signposts in the Bend of the Boyne point the way to **Ledwidge's House.** They bring you from the narrow byways to the road for Slane and, of course, to the birthplace and home of the poet. It is a neat, semi-detached cottage of stone with a slate roof, one of many similar dwellings built for workers on the great estate. Francis Ledwidge had established himself as a major poet before his death in action in the First World War at the age of thirty. The house is a lovely place to stop. Even if you have had enough museums, enjoy a walk around the old orchard and one more prospect of the river.

The road passes straight through **Slane,** and goes along by the high stone wall of **Slane Castle,** best known these days as the site of monster pop-concerts but also very welcoming with meals and conducted tours in between. The road runs high above the valley, the river keeping tantalisingly out of sight below on the left. It passes **Donaghmore** whose round tower was the site of a particularly gruesome incident when frustrated foreigners, failing to extract the monks, burned them instead.

In the town of **Navan** go beside the Boyne for a while on the main road to Dublin, and then turn off to the right, just before the lovely stone bridge in the direction of **Kilmessan.** Follow the road

for **Trim** which crosses the Boyne once more and brings you to **Bective Abbey,** a magnificent collection of grey stone buildings under the guardianship of a great beech tree. Bective was founded in the 12th century, enlarged and rebuilt in later years and finally turned into a great fortified mansion. Erudite visitors can have a feast of identifying architectural styles within: normal mortals have a lovely time exploring the towers and spiral staircases.

From Bective it is not too far to the wonderful town of **Trim** with its superb castle, narrow streets and numerous ancient churches and modern restaurants.

But if you need to head for home at this stage continue up the road from Bective and turn right to go back to Navan, cross the river and go eastwards, passing Slane on the left to make a final stop at **Rosnaree.**

There is nothing very much to tell you that you have arrived at Rosnaree, the burial place of the great king Cormac MacAirt. But there is an old mill house at the bottom of the hill beside the river and, to the left of its door, almost obliterated by whitewash, a Sheelanagig. Sheelanagigs are faintly indecent female-figures carved in stone. Many people have photographed them, described them in learned journals and catalogued them. But nobody yet knows who made them or why.

As far as the Boyne is concerned you are nearly back where you started. One more diversion is recommended, to **Duleek,** with its delightful village green and rather decayed old churchyard. In the latter unprepossessing surroundings stands a small but beautiful Celtic cross. That marks the end of a tour of the Boyne Valley that can be comfortably fitted into a summer's day trip from Dublin. It is better to give the Boyne one day than never to see it at all — but you would find it very easy to spend a week there and still have more unknown places to visit.

| Distances | km | miles |
| --- | --- | --- |
| Dublin – Drogheda | 48 | 30 |
| Drogheda – Oldbridge | 10 | 6 |
| Oldbridge – Knowth | 14 | 9 |
| Knowth – Donaghmore | 24 | 15 |
| Donaghmore – Bective | 24 | 15 |
| Bective – Trim | 14 | 9 |
| Trim – Rosnaree | 48 | 30 |
| Rosnaree – Duleek | 18 | 11 |
| Duleek – Dublin | 51 | 32 |
| Round trip from Dublin | 251 | 157 |

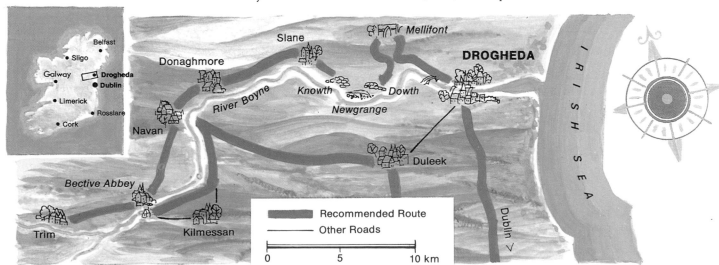

Recommended Route
Other Roads

0     5     10 km

*Highlights: Drumshanbo* village amongst lakes large and small. *Lough Scur* an island castle and a collection of 'crannogs', ancient lake dwellings. *Ballinamore and Ballyconnell Canal* old waterway linking Erne and Shannon rivers, restored in 1990s. Dolmens, passage graves and old monastery at *Fenagh*. Great demesne of *Florencecourt* with 18th century mansion and nearby caverns. Two beautiful lakes at *Blacklion*. Remote and beautiful source of the River Shannon at *Shannon Pot*. Iron age fortification, the *Black Pig's Race* at *Dowra*.

*Slieveanieran – the Iron Mountain – lies at the centre of some of the most ruggedly beautiful and least known regions of Ireland. Definitely a place for wanderers who wish for a while to keep clear of crowds and fast traffic, its attractions lie in the narrow, twisted roads, small farmsteads, towering mountains and lowlands with a scattering of silent, reed-fringed lakes.*

# Byways of LEITRIM

Our journey begins in the village of **Drumshanbo** whose name people translate as 'the ridge of the old cow', which has far more possibilities than the official translation: 'the ridge of the old huts'. Anyway, it is a pleasant village where many roads meet on the hillside and the downhill ones take you to the shores of the enormous, wedge-shaped **Lough Allen**. Pike and roach and bream and other fish abound there and that is why Drumshanbo has plenty of good guesthouses and makes a very comfortable place to stay.

The route goes south-westwards over the hills in the direction of **Ballinamore** until you meet **Lough Scur,** where you could easily be tempted to stop for a lakeside picnic. You can sit and contemplate its islands: one with a ruined castle, another with the remains of a square tower and a collection of crannogs, the islands which Iron Age families built as foundations for safe dwellings.

The little hills around are called 'drumlins' and are made up of gravel and clay, scattered by a great ice sheet which moved southwards around the mountains. Their greatest contribution to the Irish landscape was to dam any rivers they met and create endless little lakes.

Turn right at **Lough Scur** to take the road for **Keshcarrigan** and a first crossing of the **Ballinamore and Ballyconnell Canal** by one of its lovely stone-built bridges. A left turn at the next road leads beneath the hill of **Sheebeg,** marked in 1950 with a great cross, but famous a long time before that as the burial place of Finn Mac Cumhaill. Then the road winds its way eastwards between the lakes and hills as far as **Fenagh** which enjoyed some thousands of years as an important place.

A right turn takes you to the old abbey with its two ruined stone churches. Both had been rebuilt many times before they were finally abandoned, but the beautiful stone work of the remaining door and window testify to times of wealth and importance. Long, long before the Christians came to **Fenagh** great landlords of Stone Age times were laid to rest in small 'passage graves' and nearby, perhaps at a later time, a dolmen was built. Whether it was already a sacred spot or whether the cemetery made it important, the monument builders of Fenagh kept up their good work, erecting pillar stones in the course of the millennia

before they got around to building the churches.

The road goes northwards to the busy town of **Ballinamore** where you cross the canal once more. The canal was planned in the 18th century, built in the 19th and neglected for most of the 20th until 1990 when work began to open it again so that you may rent a boat and wander at will amongst the lonely lakes and hills.

From Ballinamore the road winds its way gently northwards with first **Slieve Anieran** and then **Cuilcagh mountain** to the left. Then it runs along by the side of a stream called the Blackwater to the village of **Swanlinbar** with its white church, a village which always seems to me to stand at the end of the road, nestling in between the mountains. It may be because it is a border town, with County Fermanagh just a little way up the road.

Five miles further on a left turn leads to the great demesne of **Florencecourt** – so generously festooned with signposts that you definitely will not miss it. Up on the left on the slopes of **Cuilcagh** a Mr. Willis in the 18th century found two yew trees which grew upright instead of spreading outwards like the common yew. He planted one in his own garden where it lived until 1865 and gave the other to his landlord, the Earl of Enniskillen. From that one tree, cuttings were taken and planted in many countries. Although similar trees have been found occasionally, none was ever quite so

fine and upstanding as the yew of Florencecourt.

There is much to see in the demesne, including the magnificent classical house, a National Trust property and therefore welcoming visitors. Two miles farther on is the fantastic **Marble Arch cave** from which the **Claddagh River** gushes out: the thing to do there is to take a boat-trip within the cave.

After the Marble Arch the road goes down to the village of Blacklion on the edge of the lower of the two **Lough Macneans**. At **Blacklion** you cross the border back into County Leitrim and begin your hunt for the **Shannon Pot.** Keep to the left in the village, taking a minor road to the west and turn left a mile and a half farther on. It is a narrow road, going past small farmsteads. The wonderful cauldron from which the river

gushes out is only a short walk from a parking place. When you look at the sparkling water on a fine summer's day it is easy to understand the logic of the Celts who believed that rivers all came from dark caverns beneath the earth.

Take the next turn right, a mile down the hill from the **Shannon Pot** and head westwards to a slightly better road which leads to **Dowra.** The steep, flat-topped mountain on the left is called the Playground and there are traditions about its use as a dancing floor to celebrate the great Celtic summer festival of Lughnasa.

Turn right before you enter **Dowra** and immediately afterwards left down the road which follows an embankment marked on the map in Gothic letters as the **Black Pig's Race or Worm Ditch.**

Nobody knows who made it, why or when. It seems unlikely that either a black pig or a worm were seriously involved – even though the worm may have been a 17th- century English one from the time when the word could equally well mean 'dragon'. Iron age Irish people, about the beginning of the Christian era, were enthusiastic builders of enormous earth works and this is probably one of them. In the days, perhaps two thousand years ago, when it was built and maintained, the ditch would have been deeper and the bank steeper, both would have been a very effective means of preventing the neighbours from driving your cattle away to the west. The narrow road follows the ditch all the way down to a very pleasant stopping place on the north shore of **Lough Allen.**

From **Dowra** the journey finishes by a long road to the south, between lake and iron mountains. Long ago they quarried

iron ore there and brought it down the lake by boat for smelting. The iron-masters cut the oak trees which grew **nearby to make charcoal and, as they never** bothered to conserve the forests, had to move ever farther downstream. There are places called **Furnace** at intervals all the way down the Shannon.

Nowadays, although people are just beginning to plant new oak forests, nobody mines the iron. So the mountains **and lake are left for visitors to enjoy in** peace and quiet.

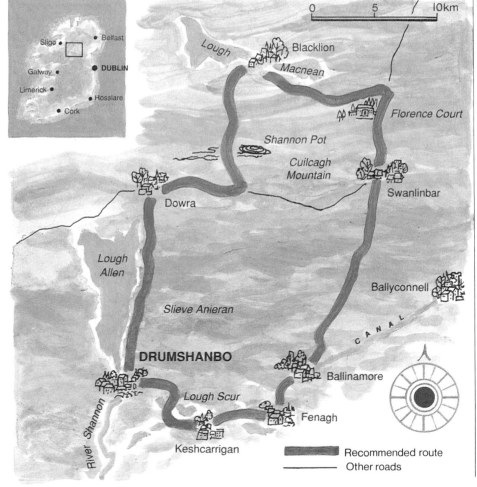

|  | km | miles |
|---|---|---|
| Drumshanbo – Lough Scur | 5 | 4 |
| Lough Scur – Fenagh | 14 | 8 |
| Fenagh – Ballinamore | 5 | 4 |
| Ballinamore – Swanlinbar | 20 | 13 |
| Swanlinbar – Marble Arch | 15 | 9 |
| Marble Arch – Shannon Pot | 14 | 8 |
| Shannon Pot – Dowra | 17 | 10 |
| Dowra – Drumshanbo | 18 | 11 |
| Round trip from Drumshanbo | 108 | 67 |

## 21 CAVAN and MONAGHAN

*Highlights:* A round trip through *drumlin* country, a land of small hills and hidden lakes. *Kilmore* cathedral town with remains of Anglo-norman fortifications. *Killykeen* forest park with woodland and lakeshore walks. *Butler's Bridge* assortment of concrete sculpture, collection of horse-drawn vehicles and a good pub. *Clones* round tower and Celtic cross. *Monaghan town* old market house and award-winning local museum and art gallery. *Iniskeen* site of old monastery and burial place of the poet Patrick Kavanagh. *Kingscourt* forest park with pleasant walks. *Cohaw* stone age tomb, one of the oldest in Ireland.

*The Killykeen signposts bring you into a forest on the edge of Lough Oughter, which is part of the wonderful maze of land and lakes which the drumlin country produces. There are comfortable modern wooden chalets to stay in or a restaurant if you just want to stop off for a meal and miles and miles of lake shore.*

# Cavan and Monaghan

Our journey begins in **Cavan** town by following the signposts which lead to **Killykeen Forest Park**. The roads of Cavan and Monaghan are wonderful things, conspiring to reduce the careful motorist to a gentle speed, in harmony with the peace and quiet of the country. This landscape, which forms a belt nearly all the way across Ireland in the north midlands, militates against any form of rapid transport or direct journeys.

Known as 'drumlin' scenery, it is a seemingly endless range of low, oval hills, few of them more than a mile long or rising to more than a couple of hundred feet in height. The hills are composed of gravel or clay, deposited very recently in geological terms: some time between 10,000 and 15,000 years ago. While geologists have been able to tell when the drumlins were formed, they remain baffled by the how and the why. The gravel was transported and dumped by moving ice sheets.

The puzzle lies in why it should have been dumped in the form of the long, low hills.

Just three miles south of Cavan town the cathedral of **Kilmore** stands on the hillside above the road. To the west of it is a tree-girt mound, all that remains of a stronghold built by the Anglo-Norman warlord Hugo de Lacy in 1211 in the idle hope of subduing the men of Ulster.

The Killykeen signposts bring you into a forest by Lough Oughter, with wooden chalets, a restaurant and miles and miles of lake shore.

If you are a brave explorer turn left at the entrance to the forest park as you leave and go towards **Butler's Bridge** by the byroads. They are devoid of helpful signposts and a good map (Ordnance Survey half-inch Sheet 8) is decidedly helpful. These roads twist and turn and rise and fall amongst the woods and along the margins of half-forgotten, reed-fringed lakes where stately swans and crested grebes sail on the placid water.

In places the byroads are very steep and narrow. If you don't like the idea of travelling in reverse for a while when you meet a farm tractor with a load of muck, you might be well advised to take the main road back to **Cavan** and find the signposts for **Belturbet** and **Enniskillen**. Whichever way you choose, the place you must visit on the way is **Butler's Bridge**

under which the River Annalee flows before losing itself in the maze of lakes to the west.

This is where you will come upon the concrete cows. There are horses and people and other creatures, too, sculpted by Johnnie Little. The Derragarra Inn and its concrete companions are owned by John Clancy who serves excellent meals in the midst of his extraordinary collection of bric-a-brac. Hunt carefully through it to find an assortment of farm implements and all sorts of rural craftwork. But be sure to leave enough time to ask John to show

you his unique collection of horse-drawn carts and carriages, the older specimens beautifully restored and refitted.

From Butler's Bridge a well-signposted road leads to the ancient town of **Clones**. That road is almost straight in parts and goes by level ground decorated with little reed-fringed lakes. There once was a canal going past Clones. Now it is nearly derelict, but some enterprising wildfowl enthusiasts have made a duck sanctuary there. Dozens of wild ducks and drakes live in safety within a wire mesh enclosure and greet you cheerfully and hungrily if you go to see them. Bring some breadcrumbs.

Clones stands, or rather climbs, all over an extremely steep hillside. Down at the bottom of the hill a round tower stands, a fine example of the magnificent bell-towers which were built in the Celtic

monasteries about the time of the Viking invaders, more than one thousand years ago. The towers were so stoutly built that they resisted not only the invaders, but also the ravages of time and of desecration which reduced the old monasteries to fragments of walls and arches.

The monastery stood at the bottom of the hill, but near the top, the next wave of invaders, the Anglo-Normans, built a 'motte,' a tall, steep-sided mound like the one at Kilmore.

The plan of the modern town of Clones dates to the 17th century with streets radiating from the 'diamond' at the centre. A stately church looks down on the people of Clones and also on the most treasured possession of the town, the High Cross. It was hewn from stone about one thousand years ago and decorated with scenes from the Scriptures. On the south face, Adam and Eve stand at the base, Abraham prepares to sacrifice Isaac in the middle and the prophet Daniel stands, surrounded by hungry but frustrated lions at the top.

From Clones to **Monaghan** town the road reverts to its gently winding ways.

Like Clones, Monaghan was also planned around a 'diamond' but here the centre of the open area has been filled with a market hall, beautifully restored recently to make a visitors' centre. Just up the hill from the market in a tall, grey house is the County Museum. Winner of a prestigious European award a few years ago, the museum was very nearly destroyed by a fire in the old court building where it used to be housed. Its new home includes a picture gallery where there is a fine permanent exhibition of paintings and prints.

Head south from **Monaghan,** through **Castleblayney** and then follow the signposts for **Dundalk.** Thirteen miles after Castleblayney a signpost on the right indicates **Inniskeen** and a drive along exceptionally narrow roads. This leads to the remote village where the poet Patrick Kavanagh spent his young days and where he was buried in 1967. The remnant of a round tower testifies to the importance of the region a thousand years ago. Beside the stump of the tower, the little church has been restored and now houses a folk museum. The collections include writings by and about Patrick Kavanagh. His grave, marked by a small wooden cross and covered with flagstones, lies in the modern churchyard up the hill.

From **Inniskeen** go through **Carrickmacross** towards **Kingscourt** and pay a visit to the forest park of Dún a Rí (Kingscourt is a direct translation of the Irish name). Like Killykeen, the forest offers

miles and miles of signposted footpaths amongst the trees, a quiet and romantic place to spend an afternoon.

Go through **Kingscourt** to **Shercock,** back again in the land of lakes. Seven miles northwards on the road to **Cootehill** is the court cairn of Cohaw. A long gallery with walls of enormous stones and a semicircular 'court' at each end, it belongs to the oldest class of stone age burial chamber found in Ireland. Built some time between 2,500 and 3,000 years BC, it was already old when the pyramids of Egypt were made.

Meanwhile, back in the 20th century, 20 miles through hills and forests returns you by way of **Cootehill** to the town of **Cavan.** ●

| | Miles | km |
|---|---|---|
| Cavan town – Killykeen Restaurant | 8 | 13 |
| Killykeen – Butler's Bridge | 10 | 16 |
| Butler's Bridge – Clones | 13 | 21 |
| Clones – Monaghan | 13 | 21 |
| Monaghan – Inniskeen | 33 | 48 |
| Inniskeen – Dún a Rí | 13 | 21 |
| Dún a Rí – Cohaw | 17 | 27 |
| Cohaw – Cavan town | 13 | 21 |
| The round tour | 120 | 188 |

Ordnance Survey half-inch map Sheet 8.

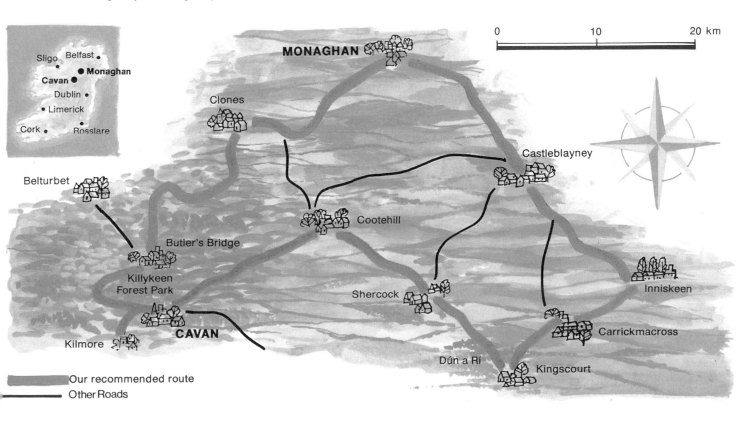

0    10    20 km

MONAGHAN

Clones

Castleblayney

Belturbet

Cootehill

Butler's Bridge

Killykeen Forest Park

Shercock

Inniskeen

CAVAN

Carrickmacross

Kilmore

Dún a Rí

Kingscourt

Our recommended route
Other Roads

The Cross of Muiredach at Monasterboice: The peak of perfection in early Christian art (Route 22).

## 22 BYWAYS OF COUNTY LOUTH

*Highlights:* Remote and peaceful monastic site at *Mellifont*. Attractive village with good restaurant at *Collon*. View of Boyne Valley and Mountains of Mourne from *Mount Oriel*. Mysterious ruins of *Jumping Church*. Town of *Ardee* with castles and ancient town houses. Stone-roofed church in village of *Louth*. Magnificent hilltop castle at *Castleroche*. Round tower and ancient cross of *Dromiskin*. Riverside restaurant and old watermill at *Castlebellingham*. Fishing village of *Annagassan*. Two of the absolute top quality celtic crosses at *Monasterboice*.

*Louth is the smallest county in Ireland and abounds in superlatives: the most spectacular castle, the most perfect Celtic cross, to say nothing of the only church that ever jumped. Small in this case is exceedingly beautiful and has the added advantage that a relatively short journey brings you to many wonders.*

# By~ways of County Louth

This journey begins in the historic town of **Drogheda** where travellers from Dublin cross the **River Boyne** by the new bridge. A signpost at the traffic lights on the north side of the river shows the way to where King James and King William fought *The Battle of the Boyne*. It also happens to be the route which leads to the very much more peaceful site of **Mellifont Abbey,** our first stopping place.

The route follows the Boyne for a little way, leaving it to take the lovely narrow, winding road through **King William's Glen:** a deep little valley shaded by hawthorn bushes and beech trees and tenanted by one ancient farmhouse beside the stream.

Signposts from the glen take you to the car park of Mellifont from which you gaze down over an expanse of level ground surrounded by low hills: woodland on the right and pasture to the left. In the middle stands just one tall building, supported by graceful arches. Its technical name, *lavabo* definitely sounds better than its translation as *washouse*. Most of the other remains of

Mellifont are little more than the foundations of walls and pillars. But you can wander amongst them yourself, or accept the leadership of one of the charming young guides who work there in the summer, and reflect on how magnificent the community had been in its great days eight hundred years ago. Historically it is a place of exceptional importance, founded by Archbishop Malachy with the assistance and advice of the great Saint Bernard.

When you leave Mellifont turn left over the river at the crossroads and right at the main road which takes you to **Collon.** Collon is a village that people usually drive through rather quickly and it deserves better treatment than that. Quite apart from the tempting restaurant on the left, there is a beautiful village square on the right, with a clock tower and small, neat houses built early in the 19th century.

A diversion to the left just before the Round House Restaurant takes you high over the hill called **Mount Oriel** which gives a view southwards over the valley of the Boyne and northwards to the Mountains of Mourne. At the bottom of the hill you rejoin the road to **Ardee.**

A well-hidden signpost to the right just as you enter Ardee points the way to **Jumping Church.** About half a mile down the road a second sign marks a right turn after which you drive for a mile or two over green hills to an im-

maculately kept old churchyard. There stands — or leans — the gable of an ancient church about a yard inside the place where the foundations show it was built. Historical observations themselves are hard enough to credit. The wall was shifted by a great storm in 1715. But tradition knows much better. A heretic was buried inside the church and the wall miraculously jumped inwards so that his grave still lies on the outside.

The origin of the name Ardee is 'Ferdia's Ford', Ferdia being the mythical hero who was almost the equal of the great Cuchulain. A little way to the north of the bridge, where the ford lay in ancient times, is a 15th-century castle and farther down the street an equally old town house, still very much in use.

From Ardee you go through **Tallanstown** to the half-forgotten and very well-hidden village of Louth which lies to its north. The most interesting feature is the tiny stone-roofed church built in the 12th century on the site of a monastery founded six hundred years earlier by St. Mochta, a disciple of St. Patrick and, like him, a British emigrant. The ruins of an enormous church, together with the fact that the whole county is named after it, show that Louth had known better days.

The road northwestwards from Louth passes close to **Cloghafarmore,** 'The stone of the big man', a pillar stone to which, tradition tells, Cuchulain tied himself when mortally wounded so that he could die on his feet, facing his enemies. Sadly, the stone is not signposted and keeps itself rather to itself —

unlike the next monument which, though one of the least-known, makes a fair claim for being the most spectacular of all the castles of Ireland.

You find it by turning left in **Knockbridge** and heading straight on over all the crossroads for the next five miles. Then you see on the right the magnificent twin towers and walls of **Castleroche,** occupying an entire hilltop and commanding a marvellous view of the rolling land beneath it. It was built, the story goes, in 1236 by an aggressive lady named Rohesia de Verdun. She offered the architect her hand in marriage but avoided the union by having him thrown out of the window. The strength

of the walls which have stood there for seven hundred years testify to his skill.

Following the road past the castle takes you quickly to **Dundalk** where the route takes a diversion in the direction of Ardee, leaving it a little more than two miles to the south where a signpost points to **Castlebellingham.** At **Dromiskin** stands one of the smallest

Round Towers in Ireland and a cross with little carvings of a hunting scene and various strange animals.

In Castlebellingham you might be tempted to stop at the riverside restaurant with its old watermill, after which the route crosses the main road to go through the little fishing village of **Annagassan.** Then head southwards until a signpost to **Fieldstown** directs you back to the main road where a sign for the Boyne Drive shows the way to our final stopping place of **Monasterboice.**

Little remains there of what must have been one of the greatest centres of the arts a thousand years ago. But the little is worth going a long way to see. The centrepiece is the Cross of Muiredach, one of the most beautiful and best preserved of all the great Celtic crosses. Take a long time to study it: ideally bring a handbook with you to identify all the sculptures. Although engaged in a serious work of religious art, the sculptor never concealed his sense of fun. So he embellished his cross with cats and gnomes and other unlikely beings. And he did a particularly vivid scene of the Last Judgement in which enthusiastic devils propel the damned to the infernal regions.

But you should banish their gloomy message from your thoughts and set off home across the green fields, continuing on the road past Monasterboice. Turn left at the next junction and right immediately afterwards for just one more narrow road over a hill and one more view of the plains before the journey ends in **Drogheda.**

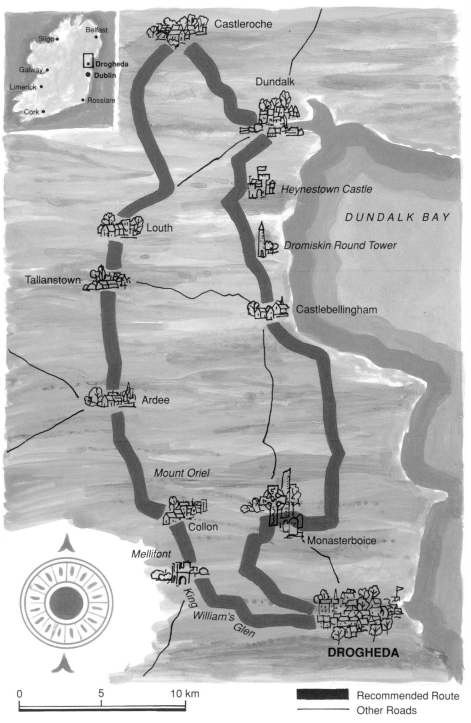

| Distances | km | miles |
|---|---|---|
| (Dublin to Drogheda) | 48 | 30 |
| Drogheda – Mellifont | 11 | 7 |
| Mellifont – Jumping Church | 19 | 12 |
| Jumping Church – Ardee | 3 | 2 |
| Ardee – Louth | 11 | 7 |
| Louth – Castleroche | 16 | 10 |
| Castleroche – Dromiskin | 19 | 12 |
| Dromiskin – Monasterboice | 26 | 16 |
| Monasterboice – Drogheda | 11 | 7 |
| (Drogheda to Dublin) | 48 | 30 |
| | — | — |
| Round trip in Co. Louth | 116 | 73 |
| Round trip from Dublin | 212 | 133 |

## 23 A DIVERTING WAY TO WEXFORD

*Highlights:* Village of *Blessington* (see Route 38), followed by *Pollaphuca* with spectacular gorge of the River Liffey and remarkable stone bridges. After *Baltinglass* the road follows the valley of the River Slaney. Old mill and pleasant restaurant at *Rathvilly*. Site of bronze age settlement and great stone circles at *Rathgall*. Beautiful garden at *Altamont* leading down to the Slaney. Church with windows by Evie Hone at *Myshall*. *Clohamon House* at *Bunclody* stately home with possibility of dining and staying in lovely surroundings. Numerous ruined castles and churches at *Ferns*, palace of the McMurrough kings of old. Museum in castle at *Enniscorthy.*

*This is a dangerous way to go to Wexford. I set off one fine May morning but I never got to Wexford, not even as far as Enniscorthy. There were so many beguiling places and charming people on the way that a two and a half hour trip somehow extended through the length of the day, and I still hadn't seen the half of it.*

# A diverting way to Wexford

The route follows the wonderful chain of mountains which runs near the coast nearly all the way to Wexford. At the edges of the suburbs of **Dublin** you climb steeply up the hillside between Tallaght and Brittas, leaving the great plains of Dublin and the north behind you. On a clear day you can see the Mountains of Mourne.

We are not allowed to stop in **Blessington** because I have already written about it: just whizz through its stately main street, past the 17th century church and the homely Downshire Hotel until you come to the stone bridge which spans the magnificent gorge of **Pollaphuca.**

Here, in days gone by, Dublin's river, the Liffey, used to hurl herself down a trio of cascades. The Electricity Supply Board captured her in the 1940s and now she flows discreetly through a man-made cavern. Stop and gaze over the bridge in both directions, and go through the little gate to admire the bridge itself. It was designed by Alexander Nimmo in the 1820s and, like many of the bridges on the Liffey, it's a work of art, not just a brilliant feat of engineering. Nimmo must have felt that so splendid a gorge deserved something more than a simple arch, so he added turrets and things to make it look like a medieval castle.

Then drive in on the right to Poulaphouca House. If you walk back along its avenue, you will see the extraordinary Dry Bridge which spans an equally dry valley: obviously a river valley, but abandoned thousands of years ago by the capricious Anna Liffey. Alternatively, walk on past the pleasant pub, through the little stable yard and find a path which brings you gently down into the gorge where the Liffey flows.

As you drive southwards, along the floor of another valley abandoned by its stream, you leave the Liffey and enter the realm of the Slaney, a beautiful river whose course you follow all the way to **Wexford** where it meets the sea. The Slaney first makes its presence felt at **Baltinglass** where a mill dam creates a pleasant pond, which you look across to see the ruins of the Cistercian Abbey.

There are ruined abbeys with rather more complete traces; in fact **Baltinglass** offers little more than a single row of arches. But it is enough to give the feel of the place and delightful little details have survived eight hundred years of weather. Look for a quaint frog-like creature at the base of one of the pillars and for little angels at the top of another.

Then make your way to **Rathvilly** and, if it's time for a coffee or something more, drive in to the old mill by the bridge. A big black water wheel turns, even though the grindstones which it once moved have been dismantled. The owners keep goats on the island at the weir and are busily renovating the old buildings when they aren't engaged in serving friendly meals.

The road moves away from the river for a little to go to the market town of **Tullow** whose narrow streets climb up and down the edges of the valley. Make a diversion there by following the signpost for **Shillelagh** (yes, there really is a place of that name) and find a narrow lane up hill to the incredible **Rathgall**. It was a factory two and a half thousand years ago

| Distances | miles | km |
|---|---|---|
| Dublin – Pollaphuca | 22 | 35 |
| Pollaphuca – Baltinglass | 14 | 22 |
| Baltinglass – Altamont | 15 | 24 |
| Altamont – Clohamon House | 9 | 14 |
| Clohamon House – Enniscorthy | 12 | 19 |
| Enniscorthy – Wexford | 14 | 23 |
| | 86 | 137 |

where bronze-age smiths worked. Then it was a royal palace and now three great stone walls encircle a green sward, kept mown by rabbits. Even if the lonely ramparts fail to move you with visions of Celtic queens and princes, the view of distant mountains and plains will reward your efforts.

After passing the crossroads south of **Tullow** look for signposts to **Altamont.** If you are travelling on a Sunday just go along but otherwise be sure to phone Mrs. North and ask if you may visit her gardens. There is a charming house of great age and, of course, a lovely garden. There are many beautiful houses and gardens in Ireland but there is nothing quite like Altamont.

Beyond the formal garden, footpaths bring you by a clear stream to an enchanting hidden valley. Ancient oak trees cast a gentle shade, velvety mosses cover the harshness of the colossal boulders of granite which tower above the stream. The only sound is the music of the birds. Mrs. North tends the glen lovingly, keeping the paths open, removing the brambles and planting rare and beautiful trees and shrubs. It is a fairy-tale world and I found it hard to tear myself away.

But I did, and made a small diversion to **Myshall** to see the curious 19th century Adelaide Memorial Church, a small but tall mock-Gothic building with lovely windows by the great stained glass artist Evie Hone.

Back in the Slaney valley you go over the river by the beautiful stone bridge of **Bunclody,** and down the road to **Clohamon House.** There Lady Levinge welcomes guests who book in advance to

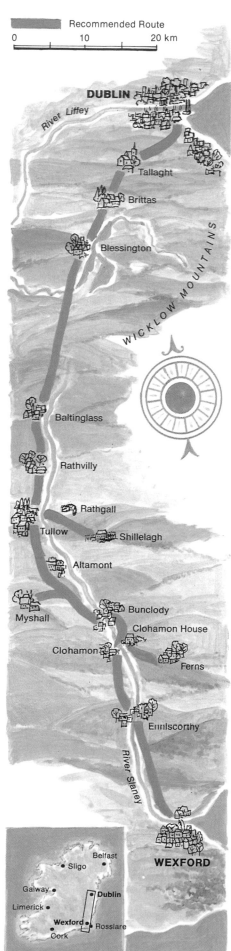

have dinner, become part of the family and spend the night in bedrooms which look out over gardens and fields and farm yards. The Slaney flows by, and you can catch trout and maybe see the fox who comes and sits in the field eyeing the lambs in a faintly hungry way.

Clohamon is an 18th century house, festooned inside with ancestral portraits, abundantly supplied with books and a place where you could live very comfortably for a long time. Go and see the farm, and meet the Connemara ponies who amble over to talk to you. Forget that they are prize winners, and just enjoy their friendliness.

Cross the bridge in **Clohamon** village to drive close by the river where it flows amongst rolling green pastures studded with great trees. At the next bridge you may divert to the quiet village of **Ferns** which seems to be almost overwhelmed by the ruins of castles, abbeys and churches. They mark the region of the royal palace of King Dermot: he who, misguidedly, invited warriors from Wales to help him sort out his family problems. They came and brought their friends and outstayed their welcome by six hundred years and more. The king was an enthusiastic patron of the Church and the curious tower of the Augustinian Abbey, which he endowed and in which he died in 1171, stands to this day.

Take the same road back from **Ferns** to cross the Slaney again so that you don't miss the lovely few miles close beside the river. You cross it again at **Scarawalsh Bridge** to continue on the riverside road, all the way to **Enniscorthy,** a busy town with a lovely bridge and a particularly grim, gaunt castle. Don't be discouraged by its intransigent stonework: a modest payment will admit you to view its fine museum.

The simplest and the most attractive way to **Wexford** after Enniscorthy is by the main road. Two and a half hours can get you all the way from Dublin. Otherwise take about a week. •

# SOUTH MIDLANDS

## 24 ALL THE WAY AROUND LOUGH DERG

*Highlights.* Cathedral, ancient stone churches and site of King Brian Boru's palace of Kincora at *Killaloe*. At *Tuamgraney* heritage centre and exhibition in a church which is still in use a thousand years after its foundation. Busy yachting centre at *Mountshannon* with boats available for trip to *Holy Island* with round tower and old monastery. Beautiful forest park at *Portumna* with lakeside walks, old monastery and ruins of great house. Craft shop at *Terryglass*, several harbours with yachts and pubs and good food. Scenery all the way.

*Lough Derg means 'the red lake' and there are several of them in Ireland. This one is the biggest by a very long way and, with its surroundings of mountain and woodland, the most varied and beautiful. In the days when Ireland was covered in forest, a great waterway like this was an important highway and there are remains of churches and monasteries with traditions going back to the 6th century. It is a very popular place among discerning visitors and there are a great many attractive hotels and guest houses all the way around.*

'We see a lot of Americans,' said the owner of a craft shop with evident pleasure, 'not the kind who whizz by in buses, but the people who have plenty of time to talk.' It was a good way of summing up the character of Lough Derg, its inhabitants and their visitors.

The roads are so narrow and twisted that nobody can go anywhere in a hurry. The lapping of the lake water is so soothing that it encourages contemplation and conversation while the world of the 20th century rushes by at a safe distance.

You can begin a circuit of Lough Derg at **Killaloe** where a many-arched stone bridge crosses the River Shannon as it leaves the lake. Killaloe has been a popular spot for 1400 years and more. Saint Molua lived there in the sixth century and his monastery was still thriving four hundred years later when a little stone church was built on an island in the river. Two hundred years on, a bigger church was built on the river bank and later still a gothic cathedral rose beside it.

In 1930 when a hydro dam was built, St. Molua's island was inundated. But his church was transported to safety at the top of the steep hill in the village. Tradition has it that this is the site of Kincora, the palace of the great king Brian Boru who defeated the Danes at the Battle of Clontarf in 1014 A.D. From the northeast corner of the churchyard you can see the Shannon and, to the left, the tree-crowned mound Bealboru, from which King Brian took his title.

The road from Killaloe runs north for a mile or two, keeping parallel to the Shannon and meeting the lake at a pleasant park with mown grass and picnic tables. The next few miles keep close to the lake shore, a region of reeds and little islands where swans and duck abound. Then you must leave the lake for a while at **Ogonelloe** to climb over a shoulder of the Slieve Bernagh Mountains for a wonderful view of the islands of Scarriff Bay. They look like a flotilla of boats, heading away to the east.

At the bottom of the hill is the village of **Tuamgraney**, with a small castle and a rather unprepossessing church. The church deserves more respect than its looks inspire. People have been worshipping in it for more than a thousand years.

In the 1990s local people repaired and refurbished it to add an exhibition and heritage centre, and there is a lovely nature trail through very ancient woodland nearby.

**Mountshannon,** an exquisite old worlde village, seven miles further on, is one of the lake's great centres, both for yachting — which everybody understands — and for mayfly fishing, which is a sort of mystery religion with thousands of devotees. Lough Derg holds great stocks of wonderful trout, big, speckled fish of incomparable flavour. For just a few weeks in the year when the mayfly hatch, the trout throw caution to the winds and feed voraciously on these delicate insects. For this short season, anglers gather from all parts of Ireland and fish from dawn to dusk.

Mountshannon is also the point of departure for Christians and archaeologists who want to go to Holy Island. It has been a place of pilgrimage since the seventh century.

You can make one more detour to the lakeshore, and a charming little harbour, by turning right just before you enter **Whitegate,** the next village. Follow the signposts which point to **Williamstown.** There are two harbours there nowadays. The first one is a brand new marina, finished in 1986. The old harbour hard by is one of the 18th-century shelters built to cater for the commercial traffic of barges which survived from sail through steam to diesel motors before road transport finally brought them to extinction. Most of the old-time barges have survived, converted with tender loving care to holiday homes.

After Williamstown the road moves away from the lake and heads for **Portumna,** the town commanding the next crossing of the Shannon. A pleasant choice awaits you there. If you turn right before the village through the entrance to Portumna Forest Park you can take a good road into the heart of the forest. Footpaths lead off among the trees, welcoming visitors who want to relax in the silence with deer and birds for company.

Alternatively, go into the town and turn right at the two churches. This road goes down to the lakeshore, passing the ruin of a Franciscan friary with beautiful stone tracery. A little way behind it stand the ruins of the fortress-like mansion of the Clanrickardes, the landlords of time past whose demesne has been transformed into a forest and nature reserve.

The riverside at Portumna bridge is a hive of activity, thronged by boat people from all over Europe who come back again and again, held in thrall for ever by the lordly Shannon. After crossing the river by the busy bridge you plunge into a remote world of winding roads running between green hedges and small fields. **Terryglass** is the first village on this side of the lake. You will find a pleasant craft shop in what was a Protestant church. The

cash till is in the pulpit, a case of the money changers returning to the temple!

A few miles further down the road is one of the many delightful places to stay on the lakeshore. This one, Gurthalougha, is an old family home, approached by a mile of avenue going through ancient woods. Alternatively, you could follow the road on to Dromineer with its famous hotel, the Sail Inn: not discreetly hidden in a forest, but every bit as full of character. There you will meet boat people and fisherfolk, and if you fail to detect conversations in five different languages, you have come on an uncommonly dull day.

From Dromineer follow the signposts for **Nenagh** until you meet a turn for **Garrykennedy** and **Portroe.** Garrykennedy is yet another delightful village centred on an old harbour. It has an imposing tower which turns out to be just one corner of a 15th-century castle. Garrykennedy lies at the end of a road. If you want to avoid the diversion, go through **Portroe,** a neat village on a hill nearly as steep as the one in Killaloe.

After Portroe comes a tantalising choice of routes. Following the signposts to the Graves of the Leinstermen brings you along steep roads past slate quarries high on the slopes of Tountinna Mountain. It gives the finest view of the lake to be had from anywhere. Who the Leinstermen were and how they died, nobody knows for sure, but they rest in an incomparable burial place. The alternative route is an easier road which gives you one more chance, at Castlelough, to visit the lakeshore before you end your journey at Killaloe.

You can make the circuit of Lough Derg comfortably in the course of a summer's day. But that would be sacrilege. I have spent many months by its shores and hope to be spared for years to explore it in the way it deserves. ●

**Our recommended route**
**Direct roads**

Portumna
River Shannon
Terryglass
Slieve Aughty Mountains
Whitegate
Mountshannon
Scarriff
Williamstown
Holy Island
Scarriff Bay
Dromineer
LOUGH DERG
Tuamgraney
Ogonelloe
Portroe
Nenagh
Slieve Bernagh
Arra Mountains
Killaloe
River Shannon

0   5   10km

Belfast
Sligo
Galway
Shannon Airport
Dublin
Cork
Rosslare

If you want to explore bring Ordnance Survey half-inch maps 15 and 18.

|  | miles | km |
|---|---|---|
| Killaloe — Tuamgraney | 10 | 16 |
| Tuamgraney — Williamstown | 10 | 16 |
| Williamstown — Portumna | 16 | 26 |
| Portumna — Terryglass | 7 | 11 |
| Terryglass — Dromineer | 14 | 22 |
| Dromineer — Portroe | 8 | 13 |
| Portroe — Killaloe | 7 | 11 |
| The lake circuit | 72 | 115 |

# SOUTH MIDLANDS

## 25 THE MIDLANDS

*Highlights.* Old canal harbour at *Robertstown. Hill of Allen*, retreat of the legendary warriors of Finn MacCumhaill. *Portarlington, Mountmellick* and *Rosenallis* villages founded by various religious refugees in the 17th century. Beautiful hills, woods and valleys in the *Slieve Bloom Mountains*. Modern peat workings at *Ferbane* and ancient bogland reserve at Clara. Coffee shop in old distillery at *Kilbeggan*.

*One of the many wonderful things about the landscape of Ireland is that it never goes on for too long. You can lose yourself in some mountain fastness and come out again the other side in ten minutes. Or you can go and view the bogs of the midlands, in the certainty that you just can't travel through them for long enough to make them monotonous. This bog is basically inhospitable, and for centuries people have been avoiding it except to dig the peat for fuel. In the 1950s things began to change. First Bord na Móna, the 'Board of the Bogs' mechanised the winning of fuel. Power stations and factories to turn the peat into handy fireside fuel were built. Then people realised that the landform itself was so rare as to be valuable and worthy of conservation. So, while the exploitation goes on in some parts, others are being carefully preserved for posterity. You can see both activities on this trip.*

**T**his journey is a round tour, so you can begin from **Dublin** or **Limerick** or **Galway.** If you start from Dublin, take the main Galway road through Lucan and turn off as soon as you see a sign on the left for **Celbridge.** This byway goes along the side of a golf links, with the most beautiful velvet grass that you will ever see.

The grass grows on the slopes of a kind of hill of gravel known as an esker. What makes eskers interesting is that they stand up as well-drained and fertile soil in the midst of the bog. Where there is fertile land there are people, and where there are people there are ancient buildings and modern hostelries, in fact everything that is needed for a pleasant journey.

In **Celbridge,** cross the River Liffey and turn left for the villages of **Prosperous** and **Clane,** linked together by one of the rarest things in Irish geography, a perfectly straight road. Half a mile past Prosperous turn left, following the signposts for **Robertstown,** an important place in the days when people travelled by canal. The imposing red building was an hotel when express boats brought the wayfarer from Limerick to Dublin.

Just before you enter Robertstown is a tiny swamp, damp ground with tall reeds, fringed by willow and alder bushes. It is a fen, a modern example of the sort of marsh on which the lowland bog developed. At this point the canal, with its boats, flows incongrously up above you.

Turn left after passing the hotel building and keep to the main road towards **Newbridge.** After the village of Kilmeague, the road takes you high on the shoulder of the **Hill of Allen,** one of the great sites of Celtic myth and folklore — and a spot with a marvellous view over fen and bog to the beautiful Wicklow Mountains. There is a little car park on the hill at the entrance to a reservoir.

Parts of the hill are clothed with an old wood of spruces, and there is a stone pillar at the top. The Hill of Allen was the headquarters of the hero Finn MacCool and his redoubtable warriors, the Fianna.

Precisely when they lived, nobody knows: the tales of their exploits were already ancient when the Christians first came to Ireland. But it is easy to see why they chose this hill. On the one hand it has its surroundings of fertile land where, in Finn's day, there were forests and deer to hunt. On the other, it was completely surrounded by bog which could be crossed only by people who knew its secret ways, all in all a perfect retreat for a society of hunters and warriors.

The road goes down the hill to the pleasant old town of **Kildare,** the seat of a convent founded by St. Brigid, not long after St. Patrick's time. A place of worship ever since, the site of the convent is marked by one of the few Round Towers which you can climb up. The great stone towers of this kind have stood for a thousand years.

Follow the main road through Kildare and Monasterevan until you meet a signpost for **Portarlington.** This village was developed by French Huguenot refugees who settled there in the 17th century. Just outside the village stands

something of a monument to modern technology and ancient fuel: a cooling tower attached to one of the generating stations fed by the peat from the surrounding bog.

From Portarlington go to **Mountmellick,** another refugee town, this time settled by people from the Palatinate on the River Rhine. Some of the shops still bear German names. The next village is **Rosenallis,** a Quaker establishment with an old burial ground, distinguished by the uniformity of its small headstones.

This road and the small towns all lie on the edge of the **Slieve Bloom Mountains.** The road is high enough to keep out of the bog away to the north, and low enough to avoid the steep hills. Some old castles still stand there. The rich landowners of the past felt it necessary to protect themselves both from the bogmen down below and the mountain men above.

and where it is drier, covered with soft, springy heather. If you are lucky you will hear the sharp, barking cry of the grouse.

In the midst of the mountains you come suddenly on a deep, forested valley where you can stop and take a walk along the sparkling river amongst the trees. After it, you climb again, turn right at a T to go towards **Kinnitty.** This road takes you up a very steep hill and gives a view to the right of the lonely **Wolftrap Mountain,** a reminder of the abundance of wolves as recently as the 18th century.

You meet the main road once more at Kinnitty and turn left for **Birr,** a fine old town and, for nearly one hundred years, the centre of the known universe. It owed this distinction to the presence of the most powerful telescope in the world. You can go and see its last mortal remains in the lovely gardens of Birr Castle.

out ready to be taken away and turned into electricity.

In **Clara,** turn right after passing the swimming pool for a view of one of the very last remnants of bogland untouched by man or machine. This road goes on to **Rahan** where two 12th century churches stand, one of them still in use. It has a round romanesque window, unique in Irish architecture. There are also some lovely 15th century sculptures, amongst them a playful wolf.

From Rahan go to Tullamore and then to **Kilbeggan** where you might stop to admire the waterwheel of Locke's Distillery, once the home of a rare whiskey, now a pleasant museum and restaurant. From Kilbeggan a good road gives you a choice of 59 miles back to **Dublin** or 19 miles west to **Athlone** and the beauties of the River Shannon. ●

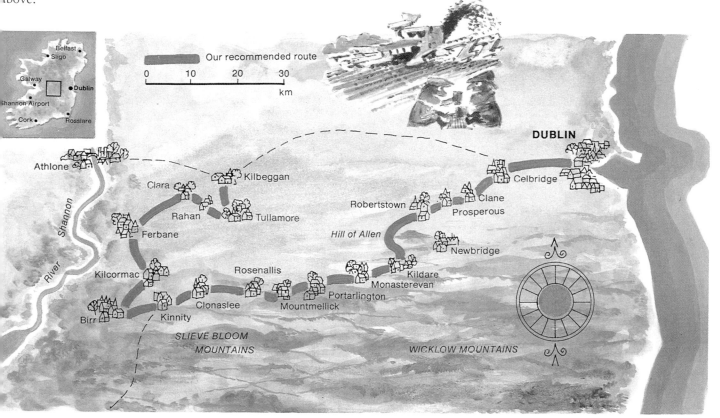

Nowadays it is all very peaceful and in Clonaslee you can take a left turn where the signpost shows the way to **The Cut.** You climb a narrow, winding road first through hedges and green fields, then through gorse bushes, brilliant with yellow flowers in spring and fall. And then you reach the mountain bog: in damp places clothed with red sedge plants,

But if you want to concentrate on the kingdom of the bog, head off towards Tullamore and zig-zag through **Kilcormac, Ferbane** and **Clara.** Here you will travel through the greatest of all the midland bogs, miles and miles of flat brown earth, interrupted only by huge yellow contraptions, crawling over the surface, munching the peat and spitting it

|  | miles | km |
|---|---|---|
| Dublin – Hill of Allen | 28 | 45 |
| Hill of Allen – Portarlington | 19 | 30 |
| Portarlington – Clonaslee | 16 | 26 |
| Clonaslee – Birr (over mountains) | 27 | 43 |
| Birr – Ferbane – Clara | 30 | 48 |
| Clara – Rahan – Kilbeggan | 18 | 29 |
| Kilbeggan – Dublin | 59 | 95 |
|  | 198 | 315 |

Birr, 90 miles (145 km) from Dublin, is a good place to break the journey overnight.

## 26 UP and DOWN THE BARROW

*Highlights.* Old Quaker school and meeting house in *Ballitore*. Superb Celtic crosses at Moone and Castledermot. Hotel in 13th century castle at *Kilkea*. Canal and old mills at *Muine Bheag*. Ancient royal demesne of McMurrough Kavanagh at *Borris*. Celtic monastic site at *St Mullins*. Beautiful modern church by riverside in *Athy*. The Barrow and its valley offered everything that people could want: rich land where sheep and cattle thrive, salmon, trout and eel to eat for variety and a highway where transport by boat or along the river bank was easy. That is why it has been a busy place since the earliest records and why there are countless reminders of times gone by.

*The Barrow is a lazy river. Once upon a time it was as vigorous as any and rushed energetically down to the sea. But for more than 450 years people have conspired to curb its ways and turn it into a placid waterway by dint of building weirs and canal locks. The ideal way of exploring the Barrow is to hire a cabin cruiser or even to walk for miles and miles by its banks along the old paths where the horses which towed the barges used to amble. But if you don't have that much time, take a car and wander up and down its fertile valley.*

# Up and down the BARROW

From Dublin a fast and pleasant road takes you through the towns of **Naas** and **Kilcullen** to the rather forgotten village of **Ballitore.** It lies about 9 miles south of Kilcullen on route N9 where a signpost indicates a right turn to the 'Quaker School.' This byroad takes you past an old and well-kept Quaker burial ground, a peaceful place beneath old trees where the simple tombstones are inscribed with nothing more than the names and dates of the dead. On the older tombs the inscriptions carefully avoid using pagan names for the months, giving the dates in numerical form. Living Quakers are few in Ballitore nowadays, but the old school and meeting house are preserved.

A mile down the road from the school turn left at the signpost for **Athy,** and left again at the next fork. Three miles farther on is the entrance to the churchyard of **Moone.** It is far from being the most splendid churchyard in the land, in fact it has an uncommonly decrepit air. But within stands one of the greatest works of art of the early Christians, a tall, slender cross carved in granite and decorated with a delightful assemblage of saints and monsters.

The road past the churchyard leads by a lovely old grey house above a pretty tributary of the Barrow, with the rather less than pleasing name of Greese, to the village of Moone on the main road. Turn right in the village and devote the next mile to making up your mind whether to keep to the main road or take the next turn to the right.

It is a difficult choice because the main road goes through **Castledermot** which,

like Moone, enjoyed many centuries of importance as a place of worship. There are two splendid Celtic crosses in the churchyard, and the ruins of a monastery on the main street. The alternative is to plunge into a quiet land of narrow roads which lead to the great castle of **Kilkea.**

Building began there in 1180 and it has been inhabited ever since. The Fitzgerald family owned it from 1244 until 1960 and lived in it for most of that time. A stone spiral staircase dates from the foundation, more than eight hundred years ago but most of the castle of today was built after a fire destroyed the ancient work in 1849. Kilkea is an hotel now, open in the summer months and with its gardens and woods, a delightful place to stop for a while.

The road going westwards from the castle brings you to the River Barrow itself and goes for seven miles close to its banks to the busy town of **Carlow.** The museum in the town has a collection of everyday farm and household things from the 19th

century. The great scientist John Tyndall, he who discovered why the sky is blue, was born and educated nearby, and the museum has an exhibition in his honour.

Take the road for Waterford out of Carlow and follow it as far as **Leighlinbridge,** but then turn left for **Bagenalstown,** also known by its older name of **Muine Bheag.** There the road runs so close to the river that you could quite easily drive in, but would be better advised to stop and look at the old mill buildings, the canal lock and the draw-bridge — and the swans. Muine Bheag is one of the many spots on the river where there were rapids and where a long weir was built to allow the barge traffic to pass in safety.

The next village is **Borris,** eight miles south of Muine Bheag. The long wall on the right hides the demesne of the Mc-Murrough Kavanaghs, descendants of one of the great royal families of ancient Ireland. Opposite the wall, on the left, are the neat houses built for the tenants of the estate in the days when the landlords ruled.

The road through Borris rises out of the lowlands of the Barrow valley and a few miles farther on climbs a steep hill above the lock and weir of Clashganny. The car park gives one of the finest views of the river, looking upstream. Downstream, the noble hill of Brandon makes its appear-ance. It was named in honour of the mediaeval sailor, Saint Brendan, who visited America many centuries before Columbus.

Below Brandon, the village of **Graigue-namanagh** snuggles into the valley where the river runs between high cliffs. It is crossed by its most beautiful bridge and on the other side stands the great abbey church, a roofless ruin when I first knew it, but triumphantly restored to its former glories.

The route continues on the east side of the river, following the signposts to the tiny, hidden village of **St Mullins.** It was an important strategic spot for the Anglo-Norman invaders in the 12th century — and they built the motte, the great green mound which overlooks the river. But for hundreds of years before their time it was a holy place, founded by St. Moling who was buried there in 697. Several old churches stand in the graveyard and there is a very worn and weathered Celtic cross. Few spots in Ireland can equal St Mullins for its gentle charm and sense of peace.

Head southwards and cross the Barrow by the drawbridge — unless you would consider a visit to the busy town of **New Ross** a little way farther on. The road over the bridge leads along the edge of Brandon Hill and back to Graigue-namanagh, giving a lovely view of the river and St Mullins.

In Graiguenamanagh turn right, follow-ing the wall of the abbey, and take the unsignposted road which goes high above the river. It passes the old church of **Ullard,** begun in the 12th century, embellished four hundred years later and finally transformed to a place for playing handball.

North of Ullard, cross the river and turn left at the top of the hill for **Goresbridge** (signpost is to Gowran), after which you keep to the western bank as far as Carlow. Take the main road for **Athy,** passing **Levitstown,** where some fanciful miller turned his tall mill building into a castle.

Athy is the final stopping place on this route, a lovely old riverside town with a castle and a market house. Don't miss the splendid new church built by the Dominican friars in reinforced concrete and lit with brilliant stained glass. Many roads lead back to Dublin from Athy, the simplest route is to return to Kilcullen. ●

**Barrow distances**

|  | miles | km |
| --- | --- | --- |
| Dublin – Kilcullen | 29 | 47 |
| Kilcullen – Ballitore | 9 | 14 |
| Ballitore – Kilkea | 8 | 13 |
| Kilkea – Carlow | 9 | 14 |
| Carlow – Muine Bheag | 11 | 18 |
| Muine Bheag – St Mullins | 18 | 29 |
| St Mullins – Graiguenamanagh | 16 | 26 |
| Graiguenamanagh – Carlow | 24 | 39 |
| Carlow – Athy | 12 | 19 |
| Athy – Kilcullen | 15 | 24 |
| Kilcullen – Dublin | 29 | 47 |
|  | 180 | 290 |

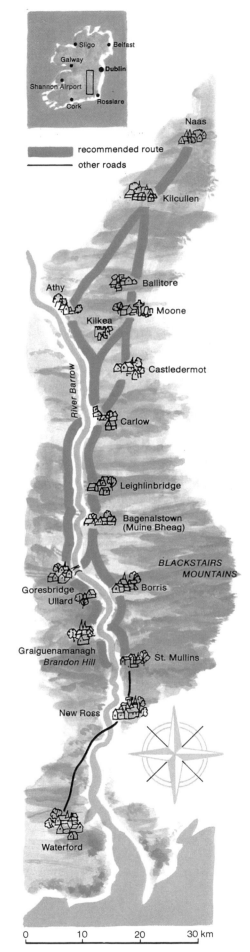

recommended route
other roads

0   10   20   30 km

## 27 A LONG WAY THROUGH TIPPERARY

*Highlights:* Great cathedral of *Cashel*. Restored abbey of *Holycross* beside lovely lazy river with old water wheel. *Devilsbit Mountain* with spectacular view from high ground. *Silvermines* with a history of seven hundred years of mine-working. Exquisite scenery in *Glen of Aherlow* and pleasant woodland walks. Ancestral home of Ronald Reagan at *Ballyporeen* and close by fantastic, cathedral-like caves of *Mitchelstown*. Green valley of *River Suir*. Celtic cross of *Ahenny* with scenes of life in 9th century Ireland. Transport museum at *Fethard* with collection of horse-drawn carriages, domestic and farm machinery.

*Cashel is the starting point for this tour, through a county which is better known by name than any other. At the same time, it is one of the least known to visitors, who normally go whizzing through it with just a stop or two at the famous places. It deserves better treatment and we suggest a long, leisurely trip.*

# A long way through TIPPERARY

Since the **Rock of Cashel** stands poised above one of the busiest highways of Ireland, it doesn't quite belong to this series. But it is one of my favourite places to explore and can't be left out. The Rock itself, with its magnificent buildings, is well supplied with guides and guide books. But you should wander through the byways of the town as well, before taking the road to **Holycross**.

Not very long ago, Holycross was one of the most picturesque ruined abbeys of Ireland. Founded by the Cistercian monks in 1180 and restored in the 15th century, it fell on evil times and was disused for four hundred years. The walls withstood the ravages of time remarkably well until, in 1971, work began once more to create a living church and place of pilgrimage.

Up the hill from the river, you may rent a thatched cottage for a week or a weekend, an ideal base for your exploration of the county. The village is quiet and contemplative on a weekday. On a Sunday

afternoon, it is once more thronged with pilgrims. Churches, waterwheels and thatched cottages: Holycross is a wonderful achievement in the reawakening of a long-sleeping community.

Take the road for **Borrisoleigh** and **Nenagh** after Holycross, going gently across the plains, past small farms and great estates, the latter securely hidden behind high stone walls. At **Ballycahill**, the **Devilsbit Mountains** stand out like a wall, barring your passsage towards Nenagh. The Devil, a particularly large member of the class, bit the missing chunk

out of the ridge and spat it out nearby, thereby forming the Rock of Cashel. Geologists, and other unbelievers, will tell you that the Bit was gouged out by a torrential river during the Ice Age.

Continue through Borrisoleigh, as far as the crossroads, 15 km farther on, where you turn left towards **Silvermines** and the road travels along the foot of the mountains of that name. Lead and zinc, to

say nothing of silver, have been mined there on and off since the 13th century. The latest operation ceased in 1983, commemorated by the great spoil tips standing out pale brown on the hillsides.

In the tiny village of **Dolla**, a signpost for Tipperary shows you the way into the mountains. It is the beginning of a lovely, lonely road wandering over the gentle, green slopes of **Mauherslieve** or **Mother Mountain**. The route is easy to follow and there are enticing signposts encouraging you to seek even more remote byroads through the mountains.

The route goes straight on through **Tipperary** town to a series of signposts for the **Glen of Aherlow**. These lead you up a steep slope to **Gortavoher Wood** on the top of the hill. From the car park amongst the pine trees you can look across the Glen to the magnificent mountain of **Galtymore**, a wonderful place for strenuous hill-walking, with cliffs and Alpine flowers and hidden lakes. A mile or so down the road, at the statue of Christ the King, there is another car park and a signboard showing the way to walking trails through the forest. Far away on the

left, the lovely mountain **Slievenamon** stands on its own. Our route goes around it, but not before heading off in the opposite direction to go through a succession of villages, each one deserving a stop and a look around.

In **Mitchelstown,** take the road for **Ballyporeen,** a village known to few until it was firmly placed on the map as the ancestral home of Ronald Reagan. A signpost in the village shows the way to one of the **Mitchelstown Caves.** It is the noblest of the great caverns of Ireland, so much like a cathedral that it inspired its owner to have a choral Mass celebrated within.

The route runs eastwards from Ballyporeen, with the Galty Mountains on your left, the **Knockmealdowns** on the right. East of **Clonmel,** Slievenamon rises on the left and the route keeps close to the Suir at the foot of the **Comeragh Mountains** as far as **Carrick-on-Suir.** From Carrick you may head for the slopes of Slievenamon, taking the main road for **Kilkenny** until you meet the first of several signposts for **Ahenny.** This tiny village is famous as the site of two of the most ancient of the great Celtic crosses. They stand in a little cemetery on the hillside, all that remains of a great monastery where they were carved more than a thousand years ago.

After Ahenny, go westwards, following the signposts for **Mullinahone** and **Fethard,** the last stopping place before the journey ends in Cashel. The village offes a goodly share of medieval stone buildings — it must have been quite as important as Cashel in its day.

The high point nowadays is the Folk Farm and Transport Museum, just outside the village. The route so far has passed by great buildings by unknown architects and gone through magnificent wilderness places. But the Folk Farm is on quite a different scale, the work of just one man who likes collecting things. He is Christopher Mullins who, with his wife and family, welcomes everybody to his treasure house on payment of eighty pence.

Inside a one-time railway goods shed he displays generations of bicycles, horse-drawn carriages, carts, farm machinery, hand-operated washing machines, a man trap, and goodness knows what else, all carefully cleaned and polished. Make sure you have hours to spare and see how your not-too-remote ancestors and their servants made life less laborious for themselves.

The round trip is 239 km (148 miles). It can be done in a day. Three days would allow a good look at the highlights but you could easily spend a week and want more.

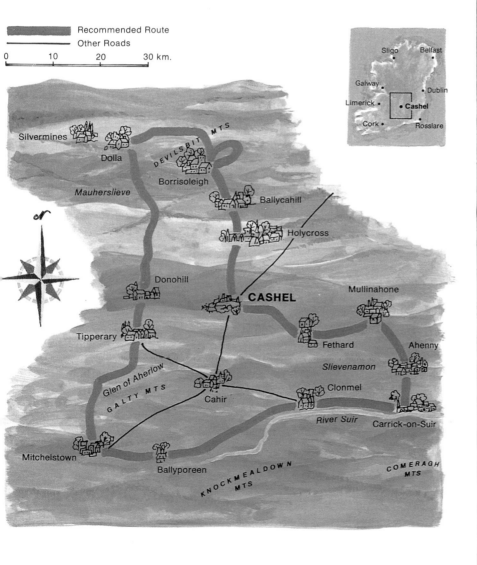

| | | |
| --- | --- | --- |
| Recommended Route | | |
| Other Roads | | |

| Distances | km | miles |
| --- | --- | --- |
| Cashel – Holycross | 14 | 9 |
| Holycross – Dolla | 35 | 22 |
| Dolla – Tipperary Town | 40 | 25 |
| Tipperary – Ballyporeen | 41 | 25 |
| Ballyporeen – Carrick-on-Suir | 49 | 30 |
| Carrick – Fethard | 45 | 28 |
| Fethard – Cashel | 15 | 9 |
| Round trip | 239 | 148 |

ABOVE *and* RIGHT: Thatched
cottages in the southern coastal
counties (Route 37) (photo
Jan de Fouw).

BELOW: The Glen of Aherlow
in the fertile lands of County
Tipperary (Route 27).

ABOVE: Sunrise over Lough Derg, County Clare (Route 24) (photo Sue Moriarty).

RIGHT: The Quaker Meeting House at Ballitore (Route 26).

*Highlights:* Dramatic ruins of fortress at *Dunamase.* Steam engine collection and annual rally in old-world town of *Stradbally.* Fleet of canal boats and barges at *Vicarstown.* Round tower with beautiful romanesque doorway at *Timahoe.* More romanesque sculpture at *Killeshin.* Market house and fountain in *Abbeyleix.* Choice of several routes through *Slieve Bloom Mountains,* home of the legendary Finn Mac Cumhaill. Quaker burial ground at *Rosenallis.* Woods and formal gardens of *Emo Court.* Church designed by the great 18th century architect, James Gandon, at *Coolbanagher.*

*Portlaoise is a town that people go whizzing through because a great many of the highways of Ireland do the same. Unbeknownst to these travellers, the town not only has an existence of its own but is the centre of a county which contains byways, rivers, mountains and monuments, ancient and modern. Since Portlaoise is such a collection of highways, we are not allowed to include it in this article — but it is a very good place to begin and end an exploration of the byways of County Laois.*

# Byways of Laois

Mountain defiles are to defend and none have been so strongly defended as **Dunamase.** The defence is one of the most dramatic rocks in Ireland, a great angular mass of limestone blocking the entrance to a wide valley. Such a rock deserves a fortress with memories of bloody battles, and the **Rock of Dunamase** is crowned with just the right kind of castle.

It appears in the distance to the right of the main road to Dublin from **Portlaoise** in dramatic silhouette. As you approach by a narrow, twisting road, the castle towers higher and higher and the rock itself is seen as a formidable barrier: a grey wall of limestone strata, in a sweeping downward curve.

A lonely church stands nearby and the entrance to the castle is across the road from the church gate. From this point the castle itself tells the tale both of its strength and of its eventual downfall. The walls are massively built of blocks of limestone and there are traces of skilfully cut stone arches and windows. The view from the hilltop is magnificent.

Dunamase positively seethes with history: it was fought over, destroyed and rebuilt by a succession of notable warlords for four hundred years until 1650, when Cromwellian soldiers made a final conquest and attempted to demolish the castle. They succeeded — up to a point. The walls which still stand retain their grandeur, and the colossal hunks of fallen masonry have borne for more than three hundred years a silent testimony to the achievements of the builders.

Down the hill from the rock, the road leads from memories of turmoil to a reality of quiet, comfortable industrious life of another age. The village of **Stradbally** is known throughout Ireland as the centre for an annual Steam Rally held in August. Worshippers of polished brass and the hiss and smell of steam engines flock to do homage to their dragon gods.

But there is much more to Stradbally than steam. The village was planned by the 18th and 19th century landlords, centred on mill-buildings and malt-houses with their quaint chimneys. The wide main street is lined with neat houses. Nineteenth-century churches for Protestants and Catholics stand close together. Across the road are the fair-green and a market-house, with a memorial tablet to a dearly-loved Victorian doctor. Thus the village catered for spiritual, commercial and medical needs of the community while, from the far end of the green, a courthouse looks forbiddingly down on the populace to keep them all in good order. There is no great architecture in Stradbally: its attraction lies in the atmosphere of peace and a well-ordered prosperity. And, lest this respectability should prove too threatening, villagers and visitors alike can find solace in the numerous pubs and an inviting little restaurant.

People who like boats and waterways can take a diversion from Stradbally to **Vicarstown,** a port on the Barrow Canal which links the south coast with both east and west, and was a busy place before people built railroads. It has faded since its great days and presents now a very quiet little harbour with slightly decaying warehouses, and a marvellous fleet of barges and small canal boats. There are village inns on both sides of the canal and an idyllic picnic spot by the waterside.

Our route goes back through Stradbally and along by the village green to **Timahoe** on the edge of the mountains. There a round tower rises above the chestnut trees of an old churchyard. Ruined walls tell that once there was a great and rich monastic settlement there, but monks and

riches have long since gone. The tower has the dubious distinction of being the fattest of its kind — round towers should be slender and willowy but this one is un-

compromisingly squat. To compensate for this lapse, it displays the most beautiful doorway to a tower, a many-arched Romanesque entrance enriched with delicate scultpure.

From Timahoe the road leads into the mountains, the flat-topped forbidding hills of **Castlecomer.** In the middle of the uplands is **The Swan,** an unusual name for an unusual village. It is the centre of a fireclay industry and there are neat crescents of modern houses of red brick. Nearby are several collieries. In other countries coal and brick and industry are commonplace but a conglomeration of this kind is rare in Ireland. How and why a swan came to be associated with the water-less plateau remains a mystery.

The old church of **Killeshin,** on the hillside overlooking Carlow and the valley

of the River Barrow, provides one more tempting diversion. It stands a little way up the road from the not so old church with a big gilded cross on its gable. Little enough remains of the ancient building, except for its Romanesque doorway: but that is enough to travel a long way to see. Red stones and white were both used in the construction and give a unique splash of colour. Irish weather, even our soft, acid-free rain, has worn away much of the sculpture but in places it has survived, as fresh as when the artist's chisel left it seven hundred years ago. Human heads adorn the door jambs. Fantastic animals, all head and twining tails, are hidden away in the corners. The skill of the sculptors was equalled only by their sense of fun.

The route returns through **The Swan** stopping, if it's time for a picnic in the hills, at a little parking place with flower beds and the unlikely name of **Spink.** The next town, **Abbeyleix,** is another designer-settlement, furnished by various Viscounts de Vesci and their loyal tenantry with a market house and a fountain decorated with the heads of friendly lions.

Down the hill from the market house an enticing signpost shows the way to **Slieve Bloom,** the nursery of the legendary hero Finn MacCool. The road goes through **Mountrath** where brown-and-white signs show the way to a bewildering choice of beautiful places in the mountains, every one of them worth a visit. My choice on my last trip was the **Ridge of Capard** where a steep road zig-zags up past old farmsteads to a wind-swept moorland, lovely at any time, but particularly good in August when it is bright with purple heather and the star-like yellow flowers of asphodel.

At the foot of the mountains lies the village of **Rosenallis** where William Edmundson and his friends, the first Quakers in Ireland, settled in the 17th century. Their burial ground remains in use, carefully tended and following the strict tradition of small and uniform tombstones. Quakers believe in equality in death as well as in life.

The road back to **Portlaoise** goes through the bustling town of **Mountmellick** and into **Emo,** where you may stop to wander through woods and the lovely gardens of Emo Court before going up the hill to **Coolbanagher.** The church on the hilltop was designed by James Gandon, creator of many of the finest buildings of 18th century Dublin. Coolbanagher nearly completes the circuit: in the distance you can see the Rock of Dunamase once more, for ever guarding the plainsmen from the hill tribes, even though they no longer want to fight. ●

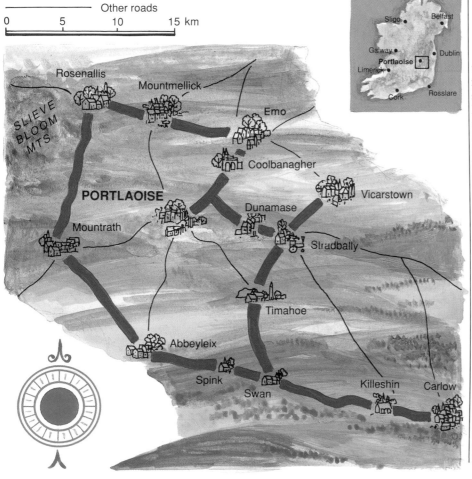

Recommended route
Other roads

0    5    10    15 km

Rosenallis
Mountmellick
Emo
SLIEVE BLOOM MTS
Coolbanagher
**PORTLAOISE**
Vicarstown
Dunamase
Mountrath
Stradbally
Timahoe
Abbeyleix
Spink
Swan
Killeshin
Carlow

Sligo
Belfast
Galway
Dublin
**Portlaoise**
Limerick
Cork
Rosslare

| Distances | km | miles |
| --- | --- | --- |
| Portlaoise – Dunamase | 6 | 4 |
| Dunamase – Stradbally | 5 | 3 |
| Stradbally – Vicarstown | 6 | 4 |
| Vicarstown – Timahoe | 14 | 9 |
| Timahoe – The Swan | 9 | 6 |
| The Swan – Killeshin | 13 | 8 |
| Killeshin – Abbeyleix | 26 | 16 |
| Abbeyleix – Rosenallis | 40 | 25 |
| Rosenallis – Portlaoise | 25 | 15 |
| Total | 144 | 90 |

*Highlights:* This is a highlight nearly all the way: a road through unending mountain scenery. Even so it does have its special places. But remember that most of them are remote spots and if you want to stop for a meal you should think about it at Glendalough or Rathdrum. *Killakee* car park at edge of mountains with view over Dublin Bay. Deep, dark corrie lake at *Lough Bray.* Waterfall in *Glenmacnass.* Monastic settlement (and souvenir shops) at *Glendalough.* Deep, lonely valley of *Glenmalure.* Dwyer-MacAllister Cottage from 18th century with very small museum. Iron age stone circle at *Castleruddery* and another one called *The Piper's Stones.* Granite quarries at *Ballyknockan* on beautiful lake drive to *Blessington.*

# THE MILITARY ROAD

*In 1798, inspired by revolutionaries in America and France, the people of Ireland made an heroic attempt to set up a republic. One of the more concrete relics of the rising, and the one that concerns us directly, is the Military Road of County Wicklow. Its purpose was to make it easy for the army to pursue the rebels who found friendship and shelter in the remote mountain glens. Soldiers seldom use it nowadays, but the road remains as one of the loveliest and loneliest in the whole of Ireland.*

From the city of **Dublin** set out through **Rathfarnham** and follow the signposts for **Sally Gap.** After passing **Ballyboden**, the road begins to rise steeply and goes by the name of Stocking Lane. Tradition has it that the military stores were hereabout and the army stocked up before penetrating the mountains. The big, white Georgian house which overlooks the golf links was standing there before the rising of '98.

The scenery changes abruptly at the top of the hill, where you should stop a moment at the **Killakee** car park. Framed by ancient trees, bent over by the wind, is a splendid panorama of the city of Dublin, Dublin Bay and the islands of Lambay and Ireland's Eye. On a clear day, far to the north, you may see the Mountains of Mourne, in Northern Ireland.

Around the corner from the Killakee car park, the road plunges into the mountains and wanders through the heather-covered moorland known as the **Featherbed.** Sheep and deer graze there and grouse live among the heather. Here you can see turf cut for fuel by hand in the traditional way. At least one of the turfcutters is a research chemist on weekdays and many of the others are affluent suburban dwellers in search of fresh air and links with their ancestral past.

At **Glencree** the road turns towards the south, passing the beautiful valley of that name and also a little settlement around a gaunt, grim house. The building was originally a military outpost. After years of neglect, it has been reopened as the Glencree Centre for Reconciliation, aiming among other things to bring together young people from the various communities in Northern Ireland.

The steep climb begins again at Glencree, leading to **Lough Bray,** a deep, dark lake at the base of a splendid cliff. A vigorous walk of half a mile or so, through the springy heather, leads to its edge. From Lough Bray eleven miles of road sets off amongst the mountain tops, with rolling moorland on all sides. In the middle of all this lies the crossroads called **Sally Gap.** The route goes straight across, taking the way for **Glendalough.** Eight miles farther on there is a car park which at first glance seems to belong to nowhere in particular. A short walk along the road from it, however, leads to the crest of one of the finest waterfalls in Ireland, cascading down into the valley for **Glenmacnass.**

Before long, modern civilisation in the form of farms and bungalows appears and you enter the village of **Laragh.** A right turn leads to the renowned valley of **Glendalough,** a place of pilgrimage since the hermit Kevin settled there in or about 600 A.D. As a hermit, he was

something of a failure: such was his sanctity that people flocked to hear him and a great monastic city grew up. Some of the oldest and most charming church buildings in Ireland nestle in the valley. There are two lakes and miles of footpaths amongst forests of oak and pine. Glendalough remains a very popular place to visit and therefore you can find plenty in the way of craft shops and accommodation.

Back in **Laragh**, take the road for **Rathdrum** and Wexford and one mile farther on turn right to stay with the Military Road. It climbs out of woodland of oak and beech, first through green sheep pasture and then up to the moorland for a while. At the next crossroads turn right, the signpost simply says 'Car Park.' This road goes for three miles along the great valley of **Glenmalure**. It offers neither monastery nor lake, but wonderfully wild and rugged scenery at the foot of **Lugnaquilla,** the highest mountain in the east of Ireland.

There is no way out of **Glenmalure**, so you turn back and go right at the crossroads, passing the ruins of another of the old military barracks on the left. More of mountain road leads to **Rathdangan,** where a right turn at the crossroads sets off for the **Glen of Imaal,** a great, wide open valley, contrasting with the steep, narrow ones of the east side of the mountain range.

Four miles on from **Rathdangan,** a signpost shows the footpath to the Dwyer-MacAllister Cottage. Take a good look at the very old stone farm buildings on the way to the whitewashed cottage. The rebel leader Michael Dwyer escaped dramatically from the cottage in which he had been cornered in 1799. It's a pleasant little house which contains a rather dubious collection of furniture and domestic goods.

After the cottage, cross the stream and turn left at the crossroads, passing through the village of **Knockanarrigan** with its tiny stone church and stopping at the Stone Circle of **Castleruddery,** three miles farther on. It is a circle of large boulders. The two facing the east are of glistening, white quartz, a much rarer stone than the granite which forms the other members of the circle. The date of such circles is unknown, but they are certainly more than two thousand years old.

Turn right at **Donard,** the next village, to follow the way through the beautiful little valley called **Hollywood Glen.**

Take the left turn in the middle of the glen, just past Woodenboley Wood. It leads to the main road and a right turn for another stone circle: the **Piper's Stones.** Climb over the gate at the signpost and follow the hawthorn hedge up the hill to them. If you are lucky you will hear fairy pipers as you stand there.

A signpost for **Glendalough** takes you off the main road once more and back to the hills. Three miles on, cross the King's River and turn left to approach **Blessington Lake.** The lake drive goes through the village of **Ballyknockan,** a community of quarrymen who work the beautiful granite rock.

Where the lake narrows, you may turn left over the bridge and visit the quiet village of **Blessington,** back once more in the land of craft shops and an old world hotel. But if you want one more journey through the remote places, stay on the east side of the lake and take the road for **Sally Gap** at the next signpost.

After crossing the **River Liffey** by an iron bridge, turn right and then take the next, unsignposted, turn to the left. It is a steep, narrow and bumpy road past a military encampment, going high on the mountainside and giving fine views back over the lake and, in a little while, forward over **Dublin.** From there it is downhill all the way back to the 20th century.

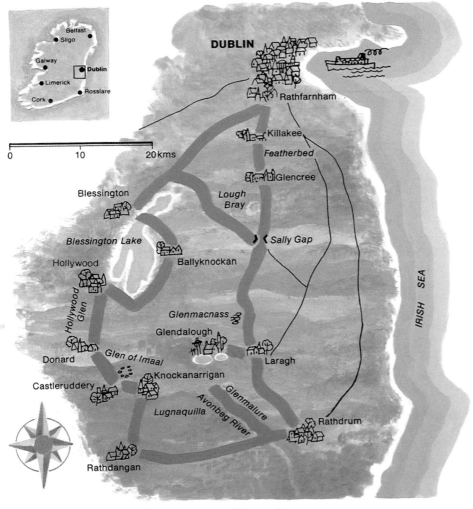

**Our recommended route** ━━━ Other roads

**Military Road Tour Distances**

|  | Miles | km |
|---|---|---|
| Dublin – Killakee | 9 | 14 |
| Killakee – Sally Gap | 8 | 13 |
| Sally Gap – Laragh | 13 | 21 |
| Laragh – Glenmalure | 9 | 14 |
| Glenmalure – Castleruddery | 23 | 37 |
| Castleruddery – Ballyknockan | 16 | 26 |
| Ballyknockan – Dublin | 26 | 42 |
|  | 104 | 167 |

*Highlights:* Main attraction is *Lough Gur*, an isolated lake surrounded by cliffs and green hills and limestone cliffs with lovely wild flowers, endless prehistoric remains including the biggest stone circle in Ireland, very attractive visitor centre in replicas of stone-age dwellings. Ruins of church of crusaders at *Hospital*. Traces of town walls and many medieval ruins in *Kilmallock*. Museum of memorabilia of Eamon de Valera and beautiful water mill at *Bruree*.

*The land of County Limerick is green and fertile. Contented cattle graze and there is a general air of well-being. There is so much rugged grandeur to be seen to west, north and east of the city of Limerick that the regions to the south are almost forgotten. Since the county is a relatively small one, this is quite a short trip — short in distance but revealing thousands of years of past generations.*

# A day away from LIMERICK

It is an easy route to follow from the city because at all strategic corners and roundabouts on the N24 in **Limerick** there are big signposts indicating '**Lough Gur**', the first stopping place. The road climbs gently to a low plateau and then wanders amongst green pastures studded with dramatic hills. Many of them look like great animals crouched on the plain, ready to leap up and dash off to the sea if you close your eyes for a minute. They all have green caps, but their flanks are often small cliffs of grey rock — indeed it is hard to decide whether they are small hills or enormous boulders. Some have castles perched on their tops; there is a particularly fine one at **Ballyneety.**

Thirteen miles south of Limerick a signpost announces the 'Great Stone Circle' and there is a convenient parking place, across the road from a lovely farmyard. Between a modern house and dairy stands a range of sheds and stalls beautifully built of stone masonry, with arches of red brick over the openings. People have been raising cattle in these parts for five thousand years, so it is hardly surprising that so much tradition should be proudly displayed.

The great stone circle is just that: claiming to be the biggest in Ireland. The stones are carefully set in the ground, some enormous, some big, some relatively small but each one in contact with the next — an unusual feature in stone circles. From the biggest, a giant square slab, more than six feet high, you can catch a glimpse of the waters of **Lough Gur** through a gateway and you can look to the left to see a smaller stone circle in the next field.

A gentle walk through the pasture, grazed by contented Friesian cattle, leads to the lake shore and a quiet land where the only sounds are of lapping water and the calls of waterfowl. The hill on the left, **Ardaghlooda,** has lovely outcrops of grey limestone: each one a rock garden with white, pink, yellow and blue flowers and little ferns peeping out from the crevices. From the hill top you may look down at an island and at a crannóg — a man-made lake dwelling now abandoned by its lake — across to an exquisite creeper-covered mansion and back down the hill to a very modern cattle enclosure.

From the hilltop, two parallel lines of moss-covered stones lead down towards the cow byre. They are the remnants of field divisions of unknown age but quite possibly built five thousand years ago by the first herdsmen. At the bottom of the hill there used to be a standing stone. There still is a stone, an enormous slab embedded in the ground but it stands no more: instead it leans at an alarming angle, in defiance of the laws of gravity.

It would be easy to yield to the temptation of walking all the way around **Lough Gur,** climbing the low hills to see more and ever more stone circles and wild flowers. That would take all day and a very well-spent day it would be. The alternative is to return to the car park and drive to the visitor centre, stopping from time to time for more wonders. Just after the shell of an ancient church there is a picnic place close to the lake shore. A little way down the hill from it a gallery grave nestles in to the side of a green hill, surrounded by clumps of yellow cowslips. It was built towards the end of the Stone Age and looks crude at first glance: four colossal slabs resting on walls of almost equally big stones. But there is more to it

than that: smaller stones have been carefully arranged outside the big ones to form a definite pattern: in any case you need to reflect on the engineering prowess of the people who could move rocks of such a size.

At the next crossroads the ancient monument looks so very like a slab of concrete that you might pass by, were it not for the presence of a little stone-carved notice beside it. The notice in itself is a rarity: put in place in 1927, not long after Ireland achieved independence, it politely asks visitors not to damage the older monument.

Continuing the left-handed tour of the lake there are stone forts built in the Viking period, then a medieval castle and finally the Visitors' Centre which, sadly, does not welcome visitors in the winter months. The centre comprises two houses reconstructed according to the style used in Neolithic dwellings excavated nearby. Even in the close season, it is a delightful spot beside the lake with footpaths leading off to the hillside.

After **Lough Gur,** anything else must be something of a climb down. But do not be deterred. A narrow road goes southwards, passing a beautiful green hill with beech trees and cattle, **Knockainy,** which once was the dwelling of Aine, the Celtic Goddess of the harvest. Her veneration continued right up to 1879. Nearby is the village of **Hospital,** named because it was a centre of the Knights Hospitallers of Crusader times. The walls

of their great church are still there and within them a splendid effigy of a knight in armour.

From **Hospital,** narrow roads take you across the plains to the **Ballyhoura Hills** and the village of **Ardpatrick** where you may turn off on the road to **Kildorrery** to find a picnic place on the edge of a forest called **Green Wood,** overlooking a valley, and an outlandish castle on a hill, just two turrets with a wall between them guarding nothing.

Then, a few miles to the north, one more place which, like Lough Gur, fairly vibrates with times long gone. **Kilmallock,** its churches and castles dwarfed by grain silos, is in its infancy compared to the settlements of Lough Gur but a distinguished place nonetheless. The great days of Kilmallock were in the 13th and 14th centuries when town walls, castles, gatehouses and magnificent churches were built: so well built that many yet remain. Don't miss the Dominican friary across the river, with its slender lancet windows reaching to the sky.

On the way back to Limerick, stop for a while in the village of **Bruree** where you may be lucky enough to arrive on one of the days when the Eamon de Valera museum is open. Even if it's not, you can

admire the old stone school building where the collection is housed and walk down by the stream to admire one of the finest water wheels in the country, carefully rebuilt and occasionally turning.

The rest of the journey back to **Limerick** passes yet more old mills and churches and castles but they must wait for another day.

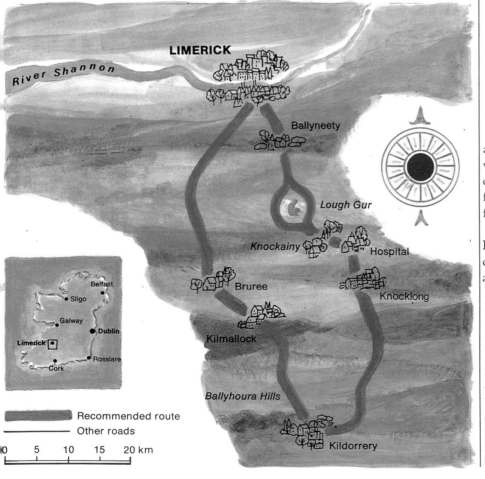

| Distances | km | miles |
|---|---|---|
| Limerick – Lough Gur | 21 | 13 |
| Lough Gur – Hospital | 13 | 8 |
| Hospital – Green Wood | 32 | 20 |
| Green Wood – Kilmallock | 13 | 8 |
| Kilmallock – Bruree | 8 | 5 |
| Bruree – Limerick | 37 | 23 |
| Total | 124 | 77 |

An easy day trip — two days if you want to take all the possible walks. Bring a plan of Lough Gur (ask in the Limerick Tourist Office).

## 31 A VERY SLOW JOURNEY from LIMERICK to CORK

*Highlights:* Romantic village of *Adare* with manor house, castle, old churches and thatched cottages. Creamery museum with old dairy equipment at *Drumcolliher*. Beautiful river Allua at *Kanturk* with poetry carved on the bridge and a great castle nearby. Remains of the home of the poet Edmund Spenser at *Kilcolman*. Starting point of the first steeplechase at *Buttevant*. Wonderful forest park, formal gardens with Kerry cows and a herd of deer at *Doneraile* and miles of footpaths to wander on beneath magnificent old trees.

*A one-and-a-half-hour journey can bring a moderate motorist from Limerick to Cork. My way takes all day and doesn't really get any farther than Mallow. The land on the byways is rich and much of it was exclusively owned by the super-rich. But they have departed and ordinary mortals are free to wander there once more.*

# A very slow journey from LIMERICK to CORK

The town of **Tralee** is clearly signposted from **Limerick** and the road in that direction makes a suitably enticing diversion for an indirect journey to **Cork.** The country is most decidedly affluent: green pastures spread for miles on either side of the road which is flanked by neat stone walls and magnificent old trees: limes, beeches, oak and ash. The peak of this affluence is the designer-village of **Adare** where I was sorely tempted to spend the entire day instead of proceeding any further south.

An old stone bridge crosses the **River Maigue** and there is room to park on the right at the Protestant church. Before visiting the church you can walk back across the bridge and stand in one of the three refuges while the traffic passes behind you and the Maigue flows gently down to meet the Shannon. Beside its bank there stands a romantic ivy-covered castle.

A little way down the road the fairytale village of thatched houses begins and there is the main entrance to the grounds of the Manor. The Manor nowadays is a luxurious hotel – you will be very welcome there for a drink or a meal if you don't want to stay. The grounds are beautifully kept, with great formal gardens and informal parkland with exquisite trees. And if that is not enough, visit Adare in July when they hold a music festival.

When you can tear yourself away proceed southwards on the road for Tralee but turn left just outside Adare for **Ballingarry** which nestles in the distance between two long, low hills. In Ballingarry there are signposts for **Drumcolliher** which is the next village on the route. But they fade away before long and I simply headed in a generally southward direction over the hill of **Corranoher** until I reached the hamlet of **Feenagh.** Its special claim to fame is the possession of a creamery which, though derelict, still displays a magnificent enamelled sign in white letters on a blue ground announcing:

Feenagh Co-operative Dairy and Agricultural Society Ltd.
Estd. 1891.

There is a new dairy round the corner,

clean and bright and business-like. But the old one is inhabited by the ghosts of the small farmers who day by day harnessed their donkeys to bring the milk churns there, wait patiently in line and discuss the affairs of the world. Down the road in Drumcolliher the old creamery building was opened as a museum in 1989 and contains a lovely collection of wooden vats and churns: all reminiscent of the days when food was food and aggressive hygiene hadn't been invented.

From Drumcolliher make your way to **Broadford** and after **Freemount** up a tiny valley shaded by ancient fir trees and over the hill to the valley of the **River Allow.** A long downhill drive close to the river ends on the singular six-arched bridge of **Kanturk.** Can there be a bridge anywhere else with lines of poetry neatly carved on seven coping stones set in its parapet? They begin by telling of the quarrying:

From my womb at Windmill Hill
Great Egmonts order to fulfil
Was brought with seven of my race
His Lordship's honoured town to grace

and go on to commend the beauties of the river, the poetry of Edmund Spenser and the joys of sylvan scenes and azure skies. Having read the seven verses and admired the magnificent copper beech by the water's edge wander slowly through Kanturk to look at the shop signs and the slightly sad, if vivid, yellow market house.

A signpost shows the way to **Kanturk Castle,** a little way downstream. The castle, standing in a grove of sentinel pine and oak trees, is rather difficult to define. It looks like a ruin but in fact has scarcely deteriorated since it was built by Dermod MacOwen MacDonagh in 1601. The story goes that, when the walls were completed, the house was considered too big and strong for a loyal subject of the Queen so he was forbidden to put the roof on.

The route goes back through Kanturk, across its two bridges and turns right to find the first of several signposts to **Buttevant.** There you turn left on the highway from Limerick to Cork and right at the next junction, heading towards **Doneraile.** This was the country where Edmund Spenser lived in the last decade of the 17th century and where he wrote much of his greatest poetry. Like most of the other settlers of the time he felt far from secure and dwelt in an uncomfortable, but strongly fortified, castle at **Kilcolman.** The castle is not very easy to find and so very dilapidated that it is hardly worth the effort. But Doneraile is a very different matter.

If you are seriously into equestrian sports you might be tempted to find a steed and race over the four miles from the church steeple at Buttevant to that of Doneraile. The first time anyone did so was in 1752 and that was the origin of the 'steeplechase'. But there were fewer cars then and no barbed wire fences so it is probably easier nowadays to keep to more sedate transport.

The main gate to **Doneraile Forest Park** is very clearly signposted – but it may be closed on a Sunday in which case you go a little way down the road to the side gate. Be sure to buy a copy of the excellent guide book. For generations the park was the property of the St Leger family, founders of classical racing, Wimbledon tennis and various other world-scale sporting events. They also had the good sense early in the 19th century to employ the landscape architect 'Capability' Brown and it is thanks to that decision that the grounds to this day are amongst the most beautiful in Ireland. That much is obvious as you wander the miles of footpath within the demesne. But spare a moment too to watch the trout in the clear water and look at the Kerry cows and the deer in the deerparks.

Go through the village of Doneraile and turn right in the general direction of **Mallow** because you must, for the sake of its name, go to the crossroads of **Old Twopot House.** There you turn left and enter the busy town of Mallow which spans the **River Blackwater.** Half an hour's drive takes you from Mallow to **Cork** if you decide not to take one of the many tortuous hillclimbs which cross the nearby **Nagle's Mountains.**

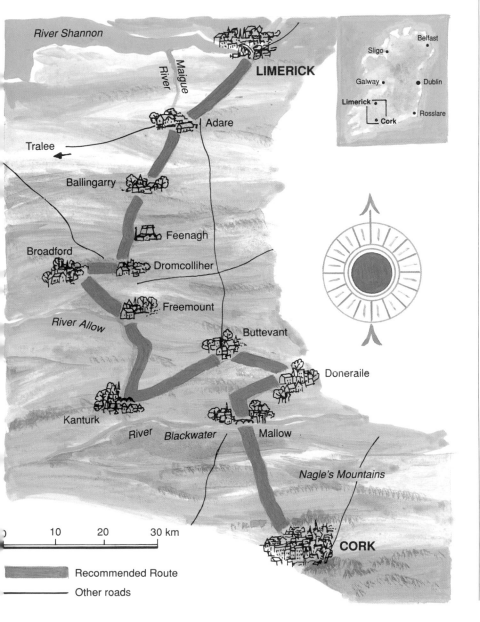

River Shannon

Maigue River

LIMERICK

Adare

Tralee

Ballingarry

Feenagh

Broadford

Dromcolliher

Freemount

River Allow

Buttevant

Doneraile

Kanturk

River Blackwater

Mallow

Nagle's Mountains

CORK

Belfast
Sligo
Galway
Dublin
Limerick
Cork
Rosslare

10   20   30 km

▬▬▬ Recommended Route

───── Other roads

| Distances | km | miles |
|---|---|---|
| Limerick to Adare | 16 | 10 |
| Adare to Feenagh | 23 | 14 |
| Feenagh to Drumcolliher | 10 | 6 |
| Drumcolliher to Kanturk | 27 | 17 |
| Kanturk to Doneraile | 25 | 15 |
| Doneraile to Mallow | 11 | 7 |
| Mallow to Cork | 35 | 22 |
| Total | 147 | 91 |

*Highlights:* Route follows the River Suir to *Licketstown*, a well-hidden village with rare traditional thatched cottages. *Portlaw* 19th century garden village. Parkland surrounding great mansion of *Curraghmore*. Medieval tomb sculptures at *Mothel*. *Comeragh Drive* with spectacular mountain views and great waterfall. Memorial to champion greyhound Master McGrath at *Ballymacmague*. Views of River Blackwater and great house of *Dromana*. Castle on a cliff at *Conna*. Traces of old monastery and churchyard with unusual family vaults at *Castlelyons*.

# To Cork by the Comeraghs

*There is a beautiful coast road from Waterford to Cork and a pleasant main road. The third route is so obscure and indirect that few Irish people, let alone visitors, know it – but it is full of surprises great and small and well worth the effort.*

You begin by taking the main road for Dublin out of the city of **Waterford,** following it where road and railway squeeze in between the **River Suir** and the steep cliffs of brown and green rock on the right. A left turn with a signpost for **Carrick-on-Suir** takes you away from the Dublin road, passing the castle of **Granagh** on the left. The wall and three round turrets beside the river were built by the lePoer family in the 13th century and a succession of noble owners refurbished it at intervals until Cromwellian times. Overlooking the placid waters of the River Suir, the castle commanded a busy waterway of sailing ships in times long past.

The next turn to the left, at the neat industrial estate, takes you along a narrow road, between tall hedges to the half-forgotten hamlet of **Licketstown.** Although unsignposted, devoid of restaurants and far from the tourist trail, it is a place of annual pilgrimage. The pilgrims are architecture students who go there to see an unspoiled traditional farming settlement. Many of the old houses have decayed but some charming buildings survive, stone houses and barns thatched with reeds from the river bank.

A right turn in the village takes you over the hill of **Corliddy,** through the village of **Carrigeen** with a view north to the **Blackstairs Mountains.** Turn left on the main road to go through **Mooncoin** to **Fiddown** which claims to be one of the smallest oil terminals in the world.

There you cross the Suir, passing a neatly built bridgekeeper's house, and turn left for the great 19th-century industrial settlement of **Portlaw.** David Malcomson, a Quaker miller, established a cotton factory in Portlaw in 1826 which developed into a major industry, employing 1,500 workers at its peak. The whole village was planned for the benefit of the workers and continues to be a thriving settlement, even though the cotton mill in the valley has long since been out of commission.

The road up the hill from the village brings you to the gates of **Curraghmore,** the magnificent home of the Marquess of Waterford. A walk of a mile and a half,

beneath ancient oak trees by the banks of the **River Clodiagh,** brings you to the 18th-century mansion. The road goes on up and over the hill to pass the family burial ground which gives a marvellous view over the demesne and away to the **Comeragh Mountains.**

At the bottom of the hill, cross over the crossroads, take the next turn on the left and, about three miles down the road, once more to the left for the old churchyard of **Mothel.** It once was a great Augustinian monastery, but little now remains except the walls of a large church and, the point of the journey here, a collection of panels from a tomb carved about 1500 AD by a sculptor named Roricus O'Comayn. The panels bear beautiful relief figures of Christ, the archangel Michael and sundry saints.

A signpost leads through the village of **Clonea** where you turn right and then left at the next major crossroads. Before long you meet the first of a series of signs to confirm that you are following the **Comeragh Drive.** The Comeraghs are the eastern edge of a mountain ridge which extends westwards for about thirty miles. They tower above you on the right, crowned by magnificent cliffs.

At **Mahon Bridge** turn right and follow the signposts up into the mountains, first through woodland and then over the moors to a car park and a footpath to the **Mahon Falls.** You can see this great waterfall perfectly well from the car park, a thin white ribbon seeming to come down from the skies. But the walk to the

sparkling stream at its foot is well worth the effort. Wild flowers, grasses and rushes cover the gentler slopes but bare and jagged rocks are the most striking feature. Properly termed 'conglomerates', the name 'pudding stone' describes them better: the boulders themselves are made up of masses of smaller stones. The nearer you go to the head of the valley and the waterfall, the bigger are the boulders. They were torn off the mountain slopes by ice, carried by a glacier down the valley and dumped there ten thousand years ago when the ice finally melted away.

From the car park the road rises over the hill and heads down towards the road for **Dungarvan,** and a view out to sea. Ten miles from the car park take the right turn for **Cappoquin.** At **Ballymac-mague Crossroads,** five miles farther on, there is a memorial not to the usual human patriot, but to the glorious memory of Master McGrath, greatest of the greyhounds of Ireland who trounced his British rivals three times in the Waterloo Cup between 1868 and 1871.

In Cappoquin you cross the **River Blackwater** which lost its way there some millions of years ago and took a sharp right turn for the sea instead of proceding in a straight line to **Dungarvan.** A left turn after the bridge takes you south, away from the river for a few miles and back to it again beneath the 17th-century Dromana House which looks down on you from a high vantage point on the

opposite bank. At low tide there is a great expanse of mud where long-legged herons stalk and wild ducks dabble.

Further south you cross the **River Bride** and turn right for **Tallow,** where some stone heads of horses commemorate an international sculpture workshop held there in 1991. The road runs along the broad, green valley of the Bride to **Conna,** a village which has grown up around the particularly fine castle which stands on a rocky knoll and looks haughtily down on the winding river below.

At the third crossroads after Conna, a signpost shows the way to **Castlelyons,** for centuries an important market place and still very much in business as witnessed by a colossal co-operative store. There was a castle on the left, but little remains

apart from its history which is carved on a slab of limestone nearby. On the right in the village are the ruins of a Carmelite monastery, just enough of them to allow you to picture what it looked like in its great days. It deserves a brief walk-around to look at the very unusual cross motifs on several of the tombstones.

By following the signpost to the Village Park and taking the first turn to the right you come to the Protestant churchyard. Although sadly decayed, it still contains some very remarkable family vaults. The biggest of them was built in the 18th century for the Barry family and has a beautifully worked wrought-iron gate, fully rewarding you for picking your way through nettle patches and tripping over neglected graves.

The next turn to the left takes you to **Rathcormack** and so to **Cork** by the highway.

A comfortable day trip – more if you want to climb the mountains.

| | Miles | km |
|---|---|---|
| Waterford – Licketstown | 7 | 11 |
| Licketstown – Portlaw | 15 | 24 |
| Portlaw – Mahon Bridge | 18 | 29 |
| Mahon Bridge – Cappoquin | 28 | 45 |
| Cappoquin – Conna | 20 | 32 |
| Conna – Rathcormack | 12 | 19 |
| Rathcormack – Cork | 22 | 35 |
| Total | 122 | 195 |

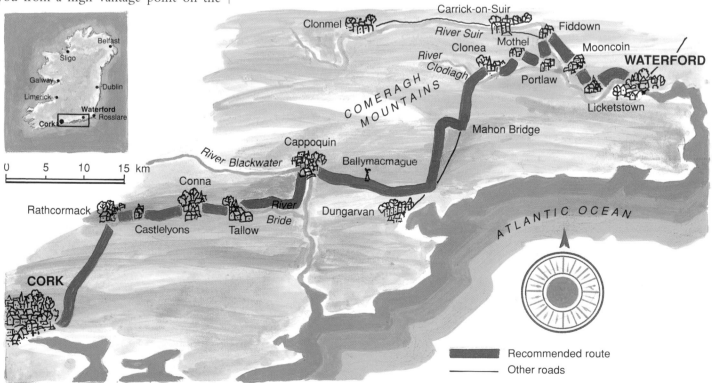

Recommended route
Other roads

*Highlights: Dunmore Cave* underground cavern with fantastic stalactites — with convenient steps and electric light. Castle at *Clara.* Fifteenth century tombstones of ladies at *Gowran.* River Barrow at *Goresbridge* with old towpath which you can walk along for miles. *Graiguenamanagh* restored 12th century Cistercian monastery. Ruins of churches and castles at *Thomastown,* including *Jerpoint Abbey,* with medieval sculptures. *Kells* priory, fortifications around lands of Augustinian monastery. *Callan* church with more ancient sculptures. Cross of *Killamery,* one of the oldest of the Celtic crosses and other crosses on the edge of the mountains. *Bennettsbridge* with old mills and modern pottery.

# AROUND KILKENNY

I f you really want to find the hidden Ireland you can't do better than to travel six miles along the road from **Kilkenny** to **Castlecomer** and turn off at a signpost for 'Dunmore Cave.' There a natural amphitheatre, a bright garden of rock plants and ferns, leads into a black abyss, the opening to one of the great caverns which extend for miles beneath the limestone rocks of Ireland.

**Dunmore** has been furnished with steps and electric light so that a half-hour's guided tour is a comfortable undertaking. The air is fresh and the temperature stays constant so that the cave is delightfully cool on a hot summer's day or pleasantly warm if you happen to go there in cold weather. Although smaller than some of the Irish caves, Dunmore offers everything that makes these strange worlds so wonderful: bright, shining stalactites with fantastic shapes and an atmosphere of utter stillness, the only sound the gentle drip of water from the roof.

Back in the land of daylight, intrepid explorers should search for **Clara Castle,** a tall, gloomy and unkempt ruin of a tower house built in the 15th century. You reach it by following a succession of lovely narrow winding roads between tall green hedges and you will definitely need a map

(Ordnance Survey Sheet 19) on which the castle is marked four and a half miles east of Kilkenny. The next stop, at **Gowran,** lies on the main road from Kilkenny to Carlow. The old ruined church there contains a number of ancient tombstones, including two very fine life-size effigies of ladies in 15th-century dress.

From Gowran you continue eastwards to cross the River Barrow at **Goresbridge.** It is a lovely, lazy river which exists purely for pleasure: welcoming fisherfolk, boat owners and picnickers. The towpaths, built in the old days when horses pulled the boats, have been well maintained so that you can walk for miles along the lonely riverside.

After Goresbridge the route goes high above the river, giving wonderful views in places, to bring you to **Graiguena-managh.** It boasts one of the most beautiful of all the bridges on the **Barrow** and has a wide quay on the right bank where you can stop and picnic and feed the swans. Duiske Abbey, first built by Cistercian monks nearly eight hundred years ago, dominates the town and after many years in a more or less ruined state has been restored as a parish church.

A steep climb through the town in the direction of New Ross takes you over the shoulder of Brandon Hill before descending to the next river, the Nore, in its steep, narrow valley with woodland on both sides. Like the barrow, the **Nore** runs through fertile land and in ancient times formed one of the main routes bringing the invading Anglo-Normans into the country. At all the main crossings the war lords built stone castles, and monks, usually under their protection, built monasteries. Those at **Inistioge** left few traces, but the next village, **Thomastown,** more than makes up for the lack. You could spend a day there easily, but if time is a problem you must go quickly through the village, taking the road for Waterford and stopping just a mile to the southwest at Jerpoint Abbey, one of the most imposing of all the ancient monasteries of Ireland.

Just enough is left of the walls to give an impression of its former glories and, much more importantly, of its tasteful decadence. The Cistercians who built it eight hundred years ago followed an extremely strict rule which did not encourage anything so worldly as ornate tombs or even a tower for their church. In the course of the

centuries this austerity was relaxed, so that the church building contains a tower with an excellent view from the top. What is more, skilled sculptors somehow invaded the precincts and their work remains to this day, including many of the finest examples of 14th- and 15th-century figure carvings to be seen in Ireland. Look out in particular for the tombs beneath the tower and the figures adorning the cloister pillars.

After Jerpoint, go a little way south on the road to Waterford, then take the right turn following signposts for **Stonyford** and **Kells** where Augustinian monks built a priory to rival Jerpoint in scale. (This is not, by the way, the Kells that the famous gospel book is named after). The monks had a feeling of insecurity and surrounded their lands by a marvellous curtain wall, with strong towers at strategic intervals. It looks very much more like a fortress than a place of worship.

The next village is **Callan** which, like all the others in the region, developed around older churches and monasteries. There are several worthy ruins there, the most convenient being St. Mary's Church on the main street on the left. Its walls were well built and have stood up to the ravages of time remarkably well but its best features are the small sculptures which adorn doorways and tombs. What looks like a particularly fierce three-tailed dragon guards the south doorway, but on close inspection you can see that he is quite harmless, being content with eating the vine leaves which the sculptor kindly provided.

Lying five miles south of Callan on the road to Clonmel, **Killamery** scarcely merits the name of a village. But the view as you approach it is one of the loveliest in Ireland, looking southwards over the forested slopes of **Slievenamon**. A signpost on the left at Killamery shows the way up the hill and down a muddy lane to the churchyard where stands a rather worn and weathered cross with splendidly fierce animals around its face.

It is one of an extraordinary group of crosses which were carved on Slievenamon in the Dark Ages. They undoubtedly were associated with monasteries, but in many cases practically no traces remain of the foundations nor are there written records of the monks who had the crosses made. If you have an hour to spare go on towards the south to see more of them at **Ahenny** and **Kilkeeran**. Otherwise go on up the hill past Killamery through Windgap and **Knocktopher** and back to the main road at Thomastown.

It is a short trip from Thomastown to Kilkenny, but you must make one more stop on the way, at **Bennettsbridge** where the Nore is dammed by a V-shaped weir turning its upper part into a placid mill-pond. It was an important place in the days when water power was needed to grind corn but mills and millers now have been given place to potters and other craft-workers, several of them descended from the mill owners of the past. After so much of antiquity, the shops of the craftworkers give an outstanding opportunity to gather some of the best products of the present.

| | miles | km |
| --- | --- | --- |
| Kilkenny – Dunmore | 7 | 11 |
| Dunmore – Clara Castle | 7 | 12 |
| Clara Castle – Gowran | 7 | 8 |
| Gowran – Graiguenamanagh | 8 | 13 |
| Graiguenamanagh – Inistioge | 6 | 9 |
| Inistioge – Jerpoint | 6 | 9 |
| Jerpoint – Kells | 5 | 8 |
| Kells – Callan | 5 | 8 |
| Callan – Killamery | 5 | 8 |
| Killamery – Bennettsbridge | 19 | 30 |
| Bennettsbridge – Kilkenny | 5 | 8 |
| | 77 | 124 |

LEFT: The River Suir at Ardfinnan (Route 27) (photo Jan de Fouw).

BELOW: The lowlands of County Kilkenny from the slopes of Mount Leinster (Route 33) (photo Jan de Fouw).

OPPOSITE: The waterfall between the lakes in the valley of Glendalough (Route 37).

# AWAY FROM DUBLIN

## 34 DUBLIN TO GALWAY BAY

*Highlights:* *Chapelizod*, the home of Tristram's fair Isolde. Canal bank at *Leixlip* with mini nature reserve. University town of *Maynooth*. Castles of *Donadea* and *Carbury*. Peatlands of *Rhode* and *Ferbane*. Old distillery and waterwheel and new roadside cafe at Kilbeggan. Incomparable *Clonmacnois*, ancient holy place and burial ground of kings. Stone fort to repel the armies of Napoleon at *Shannonbridge*. More castles at *Kilconnell* and *Athenry*. Important nature reserve at *Rahasane* and graves of 18th century Gaelic poets at *Killeeneen* and oysterbeds and seafood at *Clarinbridge*.

*'Twas down by Anna Liffey my love and I did stray . . .'* The journey of Anna Liffey, the River Liffey, through Dublin to the sea begins on Kippure Mountain which you can see from the centre of the city. The source of the river is just fourteen miles from its mouth in Dublin Bay, but Anna Liffey has more sense than to make a direct journey, and it takes her all of seventy-six miles to reach her destination. We will begin our journey to Galway by following the way of the river and continue it by taking her example of carefully avoiding any routes which might lead directly to anywhere.

# DUBLIN to GALWAY BAY

From the city of **Dublin** you follow the river, passing by the grey stone wall built two hundred years ago to keep the deer in the great Phoenix Park. In **Chapelizod,** the chapel of Iseult or Isolde who was wooed by King Arthur's knight, Sir Tristram, go straight ahead where the main road swings to the left. This brings you over Knockmaroon Hill and then descends to the Liffey side. The region is known as the Strawberry Beds and in the past Dubliners would walk there on a Sunday afternoon to buy the strawberries which were grown on the sunny slopes of the valley.

You cross the Liffey at **Lucan,** and once again at **Leixlip,** a town whose name comes from the Viking words meaning 'Salmon leap'. Immediately after the houses of Leixlip you cross the Royal Canal and just beside the bridge on the right there is a pleasant stopping place by it banks. People have been calling there since the 18th century when they gathered to bathe in the mineral springs. Besides the old stone-built baths there is much to look at. The canal crosses the River Rye on a great aqueduct. On the slopes of the Rye valley there is a small nature reserve, centred on the marshes where wild orchids bloom in summer.

From the canal bank to **Maynooth** the main road is a pleasant one, passing by the splendid trees which line the edge of the great private estate of Carton, once the home of the Dukes of Leinster and in particular of Lord Edward Fitzgerald, one of the leaders of the republican rising of 1798. Maynooth itself is a university town and that, of course, means plenty of good cafés, by the edge of the tree-lined streets. But if you would prefer to picnic instead you should turn left just before the gates of the College to head for Donadea Forest Park, a lovely old woodland with many trails to walk along, a castle and a lake.

There is another ruined castle nearby at **Carbury.** You find it by turning up the hill beside the village marked by a 'Cul de Sac' sign. The road ends beside a church and a farm where hens and turkeys wander at will. The castle is a modern one, less than four hundred years old and probably one of the last of the strongly fortified mansions to be built in Ireland. From Carbury you follow the bog road through **Edenderry** and Rhode, over the hill of Croghan to **Kilbeggan.** The roads are narrow and often bumpy, but happily free from traffic. The land is one of great contrasts: the high ground is green and fertile and in the past provided a com-

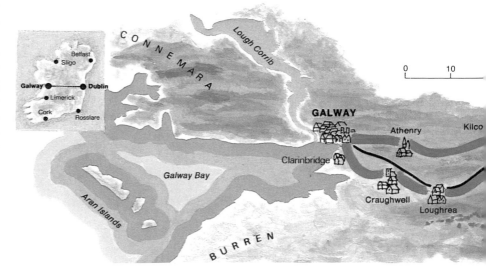

fortable living for the landlords who built the castles. The lowlands are bog, very interesting for botanists, of great importance as fuel and with a future for forestry, but regarded as scarcely habitable in the past. Nowadays the bogs are busy places, with monstrous yellow machines crawling over them to extract fuel. Nearer Kilbeggan you can see the turf cut in the traditional way and stacked in little heaps to dry.

**Kilbeggan** itself enjoyed two centuries of prosperity as the source of an excellent whiskey. More recently the business collapsed but within the past few years the distillery has been taken over by the local community who are rebuilding it as a museum and craft centre. The great mill wheel turns once more and as time goes on much of the machinery will be restored. Meanwhile you may look at the museum's collection of local goods from the Bronze Age to the present day, buy antiques or old books and enjoy a cup of coffee.

From Kilbeggan you set off by a left turn along an old bog road, first following

signposts to **Clara**, a town where many roads meet and which you leave on the road for **Ferbane**. Before long the first of many signposts shows you the way to the old monastery of **Clonmacnois**. In the past the bog presented an impenetrable barrier and that is one of the reasons that a monastic city grew by the banks of the River Shannon. In those days it was the rivers that were the highways, rather than the roads.

**Clonmacnois** has an incomparable setting, on the slopes of a green hill above

the broad, reed-fringed river, looking across over miles of flat land, with scarcely a sign of modern life. Once you turn your back on the car park you can forget the present and wander amongst the grey stone buildings, some ruined, some still intact. Founded by St. Ciaran in 545 AD Clonmacnois is a place of pilgrimage to this day. There are monuments or buildings from the seventh century, and something or other was built or added to in every century since. Take a very special look at the round tower which served as a beacon

to weary pilgrims and at the sculptured crosses with their scenes from Bible stories. But above all simply breathe in the air of fifteen hundred years of sanctity.

Clonmacnois really deserves a whole day and you could spend the night at Athlone. But if you must press on for Galway head south and cross the river at **Shannonbridge**. On the far side are stone fortifications, built in 1803 to repel a French invasion which never actually happened.

At **Ballinasloe** you have a choice of taking the old main road which goes through **Kilconnell** and **Athenry**, both towns crammed with the ruins of castles and monasteries. The southern road goes through the peaceful village of **Aughrim** which witnessed one of the most violent battles of the 17th-century wars. The town of **Loughrea** lies on the side of a beautiful lake of the same name and you can drive southwards along its shores to a pleasant park at its far end.

Just past **Craughwell**, the next village of the main road, a signpost on the left indicates Killeeneen and the 'graves of the poets'. The road to this lonely little church-

yard runs along the edge of Rahasane Turlough, a place of pilgrimage for bird-watchers and other naturalists. A turlough is a lake which disappears in summer and Rahasane is one of the finest of them. In winter many thousands of wild duck, wading birds and swans gather there. In summer, you see a great expanse of green grass, spreading for miles and devoid of trees and stone walls. The poets who were buried at Killeeneen in the 19th century were among the last of the traditional Gaelic writers, and include the great Anthony Raftery.

You pass one more ancient church before coming abruptly back to the 20th century with its signposts and filling stations, and you might make a final stop at **Clarinbridge** before heading for Galway. Clarinbridge stands at the head of a creek, the innermost part of Galway Bay, and is famous for the oysters which grow there. It has long been renowned for the excellence of its seafood restaurants.

**Galway** is the end of this journey but a beginning for many others. Beyond it lies the lake-strewn wilderness of Connemara, the wild-flower gardens of the Burren of Clare and the legendary Islands of Aran.

## Distance: 136 miles.

There is very little difference in mileage between the two routes, but naturally our 'By-ways' route is slower, the roads being comparatively more narrow and winding — and, of course, more interesting.

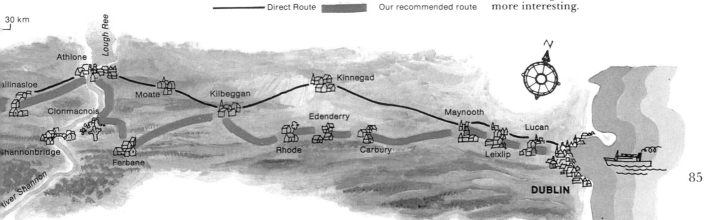

30 km

—— Direct Route ▬▬▬ Our recommended route

Athlone · Lough Ree · Ballinasloe · Clonmacnois · Shannonbridge · Ferbane · Moate · Kilbeggan · Kinnegad · Edenderry · Rhode · Carbury · Maynooth · Lucan · Leixlip · DUBLIN · River Shannon

N

## 35 DUBLIN TO SLIGO

*Highlights: Phoenix Park*, wide open spaces with trees and deer. *Trim*, medieval town with exceptionally fine castle. *Fore* remains of ancient monastic city in a deep valley. *Edgeworthstown* home of the novelist Maria Edgeworth. *Drumshanbo* centre of land of small lakes. *Lough Key* large lake with forest park where boats and meals are available. *Boyle* busy town with particularly good ruins of Cistercian monastery, including some delightful sculptured figures. *Sligo* and *Lake Isle of Innisfree* a beautiful lake surrounded by mountains, scenery which inspired some of W. B. Yeats' best known poetry.

*The main road to Sligo is an attractive one, passing by lakes and ancient monasteries and climbing over gentle mountains. The byways must accordingly exert a particularly strong pull if they are to beguile a visitor. Of course they have an initial advantage in being lonely places where you may drive for miles without meeting another car. Besides that, they offer more romantic ruins and more lakes than any main road could possibly show you.*

*Last time I tried to take the route described on these pages I got lost. It didn't really matter since the wrong way brought me to a land of rolling hills and beautiful lakes which I had never set eyes on before. And besides, after a while a helpful signpost set me safely on the right road once more. But if you do want to follow the finer points of the route between Fore and Mohill then bring the Ordnance Survey 'half-inch' map, sheet No. 12, with you and follow it carefully.*

# DUBLIN to SLIGO

The journey from the city of Dublin begins by going along the north quays and out through the magnificent Phoenix Park along its main avenue. *Áras an Uachtaráin*, the Presidential palace, is on the right of the avenue. The park itself, first a royal deerpark and still holding a herd of deer, was opened to the public more than three hundred years ago.

You may leave the main road a few miles to the north, following the signpost to **Dunboyne** and then keeping an eye

open for pointers, first to **Summerhill** and next to **Trim**. The land is fairly flat and very fertile so the road runs between fields where splendid race horses and stately homes abound.

You should restrain your desire to stop and look at tempting castles until you reach **Trim** because the castle there is so much more exciting than the others. If you are an expert on medieval forts you will be able to identify sally ports, portcullis, drawbridge, barbican and all sorts of

ancient architectural features. Even if these terms mean nothing, nobody can fail to be thrilled by the sheer size of the castle

and the strength of its defences: unscaleable walls on the landward side and the River Boyne to protect it to the north.

Trim is a good place to stop for a while, well furnished with other ancient buildings, not so ancient pubs and a variety of guide books. When the time comes to press onwards, head for **Athboy** where you turn left for **Delvin** and **Collinstown**. At Collinstown turn right for **Fore** along a road which brings you first to a pleasant picnic place on the shore of **Lough Lene** with its marvellously clear spring water.

The look of the land changes gradually as you go westwards, from the low-lying pasture to more and more hills with woodland, fewer distant views but more dramatic scenery, giving its best in the deep valley of **Fore** where St. Feichin founded a monastery in the seventh century. The saint and his followers built

dwellings of wood or clay and no trace of them remains. Up on the side of the hill, however, beneath the grey limestone

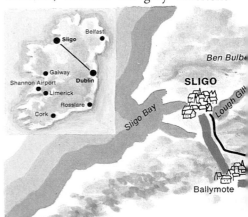

crag, stands a church whose simple doorway with a cross carved in the lintel is dated to the ninth century. Below it, on the edge of the road, a gateway is about all that remains of a great town wall but the main interest lies in the ruins which stand below it in the valley. When the Benedictine monks built their monastery in the 12th century it probably stood on an island, with a lake in front and a river behind, abounding in eel and trout to feed the brethren. They did not enjoy an especially peaceful life since they had French connections and were rather often regarded as suspect by the authorities. This is part of the reason why the monastery looks very much more like a fortress than a place for placid contemplation.

From Fore the road leads to **Edgeworthstown,** a village on the main road, established by the Edgeworth family whose members in the 19th century included the brilliant, if eccentric, engineer Richard Lovell and his daughter Maria, whose novels about life in the country inspired writers in countries as far away as Russia.

The easy way on from Edgeworthstown is to go through Longford to **Carrick,** a road which brings you close to the River Shannon and some of its smaller lakes. The adventurous route is to go over the mountains through **Drumlish** to **Mohill,** perhaps stopping for a little rest by the very beautiful and almost unknown **Lough Rinn** with its woodland shores.

You should yield to the temptation to stay in this lakeland for a night or more, selecting one of the many small hotels or guesthouses which cater for the visiting

fishermen. **Drumshanbo,** further to the north, is one of the popular centres.

If you go west from Mohill you meet the main road again and the River Shannon at **Drumsna.** River and road take a series of U-turns and S-bends which means that you cross the river twice before reaching the town of **Carrick.** A right turn from the centre of the town takes you along a back road to **Cootehall** and yet one more secluded lake and then to **Lough Key Forest Park,** a wonderland on the shores of an island-studded lake. If you like tame things you can find a restaurant and a harbour with boats for hire. But if you seek the wilderness you may wander at will through the forest and meet with deer and birds and foxes. Don't miss the lovely bog garden with its brilliant rhododendrons and azaleas.

At the next town, **Boyle,** there is a fine old abbey, with charming little sculptured figures on its pillars, and there you will have to take a difficult decision. The main road for Sligo is one of the most beautiful in Ireland, passing over the Curlew Mountains to give a view first over the

exquisite Lough Arrow and later to the legendary hill of Knocknarea with the Stone Age mausoleum of Queen Maeve on its summit. The alternative is to go to Ballymote by the road which brings you along the foot of the hill of Kesh where fifteen great caves stare out from the cliffs above. And then you come to **Sligo** where every placename echoes some poem of William Butler Yeats who spent much of his boyhood there and lies buried 'Under bare Ben Bulben's head in Drumcliff churchyard . . .'

Just before you enter the town of Sligo a signpost shows the way to Dooney Rock and brings you quickly through the suburbs to the exquisite Lough Gill with its reed-fringed shores and bushy islets. Signposts show the way first to Dooney Rock, a great cliff which stands above the lake, and next to the Lake Isle of Innisfree, a tall, rocky island covered in bushes — not much room for a small cabin, let alone for nine beanrows, but the poet was a long way from home when he wrote about it. Innisfree is 10 miles from Sligo. A further 16 miles takes you all the way round the lake to the town.

Ireland has no scenery more dramatic than that of Sligo with its precipitous cliffs, island-studded lakes and hidden gorges bright with Alpine flowers. If you don't want to be captured and held in thrall for ever, steer well clear.

**Dublin – Sligo**

| | miles | km |
|---|---|---|
| Dublin – Dunboyne | 10 | 16 |
| Dunboyne – Trim | 20 | 32 |
| Trim – Lough Lene | 21 | 34 |
| Lough Lene – Fore | 4 | 6 |
| Fore – Edgeworthstown | 17 | 27 |
| Edgeworthstown – Mohill | 20 | 32 |
| Mohill – Carrick-on-Shannon | 10 | 16 |
| Edgeworthstown – Carrick | 30 | 48 |
| Carrick – Lough Key Forest Park | 8 | 13 |
| Lough Key – Boyle | 2 | 3 |
| Boyle – Ballymote | 13 | 21 |
| Ballymote – Sligo | 14 | 22 |
| Boyle – Sligo | 24 | 37 |
| Total by the by-ways | **139** | **224** |

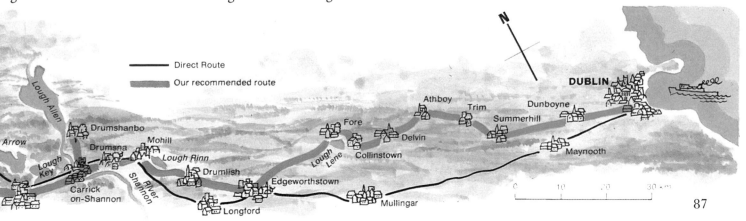

Direct Route

Our recommended route

# AWAY FROM DUBLIN

*Highlights:* Seaside drive at *Malahide*. Old church and tower at *Lusk*. Thatched fishermen's cottages at *Rush*. Old farmhouse and demesne open as a public park at *Ardgillan*. Traditional fishing for salmon and mussels at *Mornington* on the River Boyne. Celtic cross at *Termonfeckin*. Fishing harbour and Dublin Bay prawns at *Port Oriel* and first view of the *Mountains of Mourne*. Around *Dundalk* the land made famous in the great saga of the Cattle Raid of Cooley. At *Ballymascanlon* one of the finest dolmens in Ireland. Medieval town of *Carlingford* with castles and old town houses. Forest park on the hillside and old ship canal to town of *Newry*. Coastal drive through fishing villages 'where the Mountains of Mourne sweep down to the sea'.

*A fine, fast road leads from Dublin to Belfast and you can drive there quite comfortably in two and a half hours. But last time I headed off in that direction, it took me nearly all day and even then I didn't actually get there. Belfast and Dublin are both fine cities with beautiful surroundings, but that doesn't mean you have to hurry from one to the other.*

*There are, to begin with, two ways of leaving Dublin itself. The simple one is to follow the Airport signposts through the city, taking the road for Swords after passing the airport. The alternative is to leave the city by the Malahide road, keeping to the coast of Dublin Bay as far as Sutton where you turn left for a marvellous seaside trip through Malahide and so to Swords where you pick up the main road again.*

# DUBLIN to BELFAST

Four miles north of **Swords**, turn off at the signpost for **Skerries**. The land is flat and fertile and most of the vegetables eaten by the citizens of Dublin are grown there on the sandy soil. It has been a rich part of the world for a very long time and you soon come to the remnants of an affluent religious establishment. This is the tower of **Lusk** and a very curious one it is, too. A round tower was built about a

thousand years ago, but five hundred years later the people wanted a new and large church with the sort of square tower that was fashionable at the time. However, the architect felt a certain amount of respect

for tradition, he used the old round tower at one angle of his square and built three new ones for the other corners.

The next village to look for is **Rush**, a place to pay a pilgrimage to if you delight in old fishing villages with thatched cottages. To continue your journey turn left just after passing the post office for the road which leads to **Skerries** with its string of low-lying islands crowned with towers and forts to repel invaders who, in the end, never bothered to invade.

A signpost at the monument in the main street of Skerries is the first of several which bring you to **Ardgillan Park**, the newest of a number of onetime private demesnes which the Dublin County

Council has transformed into public pleasure gardens. You could stop there for coffee and take a pleasant walk through the trees and down to the seaside about a mile further on. There is a fine view back over Skerries itself, with its islands strung out like beads.

The road takes you back along the shore, then inland for a little through **Balbriggan** to **Julianstown.** Head for the sea and the village of **Laytown** where they race horses on the strand at a great festival in August, then to **Bettystown** and so to the **River Boyne** at **Mornington.**

The Boyne is a famous river, rich in salmon and the scene of many battles in the past. If you pass **Mornington** at low tide you may be able to watch the salmon fishermen in their flat-bottomed boats, encircling the salmon with nets and drawing them ashore. Or you may see the mussel men, using long-handled rakes to take the delectable shellfish from the sea bed. A few miles upstream in the Millmount Museum in **Drogheda** they have a tiny, round boat made within living memory by a traditional craftsman using a style which has been followed since before the days of St. Patrick.

The passing of time has little significance in these parts, though you will have to move into the present for a short while to go through **Drogheda**, a town crammed with ancient buildings.

Signposts, first to **Baltray** and then to **Termonfeckin** bring you back to the seaside. You might by this time, incidentally, think of finding a restaurant for lunch. But if you want to picnic, my advice is to go a little further on to **Clogherhead.** At all events, make a brief stop in the churchyard at the top of the hill in Termonfeckin to look at the cross which has stood there for nine hundred years. There's a fine castle nearby as well.

In **Clogherhead** follow the road to **Port Oriel,** a very busy fishing harbour where they land the famous Dublin Bay

prawns. From the car park and picnic place on the side of the hill above the harbour you can watch the fishing boats and gaze at the magnificent **Mountains of Mourne** across the bay to the north. The next part of the journey by the sea is tortuous, but easy to find because every difficult corner is marked by a signpost saying 'Scenic Route.' It takes you down along the edges of a broad, open bay where sea birds gather by the thousand.

At **Castlebellingham** you meet the main road once more and follow it for a few miles before turning right for **Blackrock** and one more seaside road as far as **Dundalk.** You are now on the edge of the country made famous by the legendary hero, Cuchulainn and the epic story of the cattle raid of Cooley. You can read all about his doings in a modern translation by the poet Thomas Kinsella and use the map in his book to follow the route of the armies.

North of Dundalk a right turn for **Carlingford** takes you to the Cooley peninsula where most of the action of the Cuchulain saga took place. Stop for a while at **Ballymascanlon** and take a quarter of an hour's walk from the hotel to **Proleek Dolmen,** a gigantic tomb erected more than four thousand years ago. It consists of a rock slab weighing 40 tons, balanced on top of three stone pillars, standing more than seven feet tall.

A few miles further on is **Carlingford,** one of the oldest and most attractive of Irish seaside towns. Castles and ancient stone houses look out over the fine harbour. The great bay was named by the Viking settlers of a thousand years ago and the port was a busy one from their time until ships grew too big for the shallow water. Now it is a popular centre for pleasure boats. You might well be tempted to spend a night there or in **Omeath,** the next village along the edge of the bay.

Between Carlingford and Omeath there is a forest park, approached by a winding road which takes you between pine trees, high up on the side of Carlingford Mountain: not so lofty as the Mournes across the water, but proud of being about four hundred million years older than them.

The bay narrows as you go north and the road runs along by a deserted ship canal to **Newry.** There a bewildering dilemma awaits you: you might drive on and reach Belfast in three-quarters of an hour. But away on the right 'the Mountains of Mourne sweep down to the sea' and some of the finest scenery in Ireland awaits you. Good roads lead around the mountains and others take you over the tops. Don't miss it. ●

### Dublin - Belfast

|  | miles | km |
| --- | --- | --- |
| Dublin - Malahide - Swords | 15 | 24 |
| Swords - Rush | 8 | 13 |
| Rush - Ardgillan Park | 6 | 10 |
| Ardgillan - Drogheda | 17 | 27 |
| Drogheda - Port Oriel | 8 | 13 |
| Port Oriel - Castlebellingham | 12 | 19 |
| Castlebellingham - Dundalk | 10 | 16 |
| Dundalk - Ballymascanlon | 4 | 6 |
| Ballymascanlon - Carlingford | 10 | 16 |
| Carlingford - Newry | 12 | 19 |
| Newry - Newcastle | 30 | 48 |
| Newcastle - Belfast | 31 | 50 |
| Total | 163 | 262 |

*The quick way:*

|  | miles | km |
| --- | --- | --- |
| Dublin - Drogheda | 30 | 48 |
| Drogheda - Dundalk | 22 | 35 |
| Dundalk - Newry | 13 | 21 |
| Newry - Belfast | 38 | 61 |
| Total | 103 | 165 |

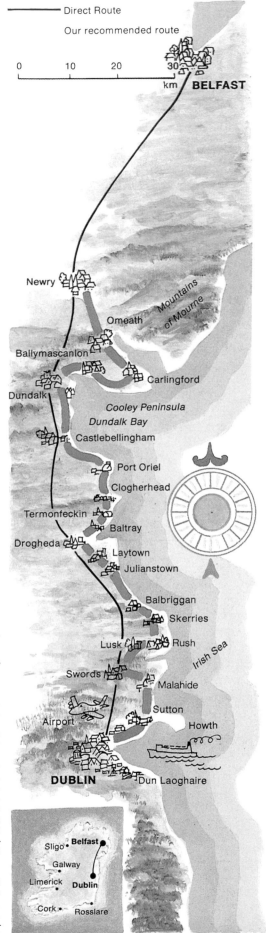

— Direct Route

Our recommended route

0   10   20   30
km   **BELFAST**

Newry

Mountains of Mourne

Omeath

Ballymascanlon

Carlingford

Dundalk

Cooley Peninsula
Dundalk Bay

Castlebellingham

Port Oriel

Clogherhead

Termonfeckin

Baltray

Drogheda

Laytown

Julianstown

Balbriggan

Skerries

Lusk      Rush

Irish Sea

Swords

Malahide

Sutton

Airport

Howth

**DUBLIN**

Dun Laoghaire

Sligo   **Belfast**

Galway

Limerick   **Dublin**

Cork      Rosslare

*Highlights:* The *Military Road* which brings you from the suburbs and for many miles through the Dublin and Wicklow Mountains, passing beautiful lakes on the way. Diversion to the exquisite valley of *Glendalough*, a holy place for more than a thousand years. *Avondale*, the home of Charles Stewart Parnell and site of a great forest garden. *Vale of Avoca* and *Meeting of the Waters* renowned in the songs of Thomas Moore. *Arklow* harbour with boatyard, followed by coastal road passing many thatched cottages and hidden seaside coves. *Wexford Wildfowl Reserve* with geese and ducks, wild and tame. Flat country in the extreme southeast, almost looking like Holland and with a windmill at *Tacumshane*. Leaning tower on *Our Lady's Island.*

*There are people who say that the main road from Dublin to Rosslare is a slow and twisty one. Others say it's very good. In the interests of avoiding conflict, my suggestion is to take a road which is undoubtedly slow and twisty and also climbs up and down mountains. It is a particularly beautiful one and turns what would otherwise be a morning's journey into a leisurely whole day.*

# DUBLIN to ROSSLARE

From the centre of the city of Dublin you can see the Hellfire Club, a large ruined building which has sat like a hat on the top of a smooth mountain for two hundred years. That is the direction to head for, passing the village of **Rathfarnham** in the south suburbs and then following the signposts which indicate 'Sally Gap', or 'Glencree' or both. Rathfarnham is the last of the lowland villages on the road which thereafter climbs more or less steeply, passing out of the suburbs, through green fields and finally to the barren mountain slopes where sheep graze among the heather.

This route is called the 'Military Road' and was built after the Republican rising of 1798 by the authorities to simplify their task of pursuing the rebels into the mountain fastness. The Military Road runs through a peaceful region now, taking you past the peat bog where citizens of Dublin make a pilgrimage each weekend in summer to cut enough turf to burn through the winter. They cut it in the

traditional way, leaving the sods to dry in little stacks before taking them home by car. After a few miles, the road begins to rise steeply again at the head of the **Glencree** valley which makes a frame for the noble Sugarloaf mountain at the eastern end.

Half way up the hill on the right lies the deep, dark and beautiful Lough Bray, one of a number of lakes scooped out by glaciers in the past. If you are energetic and don't mind getting your feet wet, you can take a pleasant walk to its shores.

From Lough Bray the road continues to wind its way over the hills to the crossroads at **Sally Gap** where you turn left up the road to Roundwood. It leads mostly downhill, passing Lough Tay, one of the loveliest of the Wicklow lakes, tucked in at the base of magnificent cliffs. Soon after Lough Tay the scenery becomes gentler and more civilised; rich green lowlands replace the brown bog of the higher ground. You might think of stopping in

the village of **Roundwood** with its great assortment of pubs and restaurants, a favourite Sunday afternoon haunt of the natives of Dublin.

Signposts for **Laragh** take you on from Roundwood, through the riverside village of Annamoe, the Ford of the Cattle. Laragh presents you with a problem: it is only two miles from **Glendalough,** the most famous and one of the most spectacular of all the valleys of Ireland. But if you go there you will certainly want to

stay most of the day, wandering among its ruined churches and walking by the lake into whose dark waters, we are told, the good St. Kevin in a fit of pious anger hurled a young lady who came to visit him.

The ideal would be to visit Glendalough and stay overnight. Then you could head on the following morning, taking the road for **Rathdrum.** This road follows the Vale of Clara, a lovely deep valley with ancient oak wood on either side. Just beyond Rathdrum is the great demesne of **Avondale.** It was the home of Charles Stewart Parnell, the 19th-century parliamentary leader and 'uncrowned king of Ireland.' His house has been carefully

restored and is open to visitors. You are free to wander through the forest park where scientific tree planting began more than two hundred years ago, and was repeated at the beginning of the present century. Trees from all over the world were planted there in one-acre plots to find out how they would fare in Ireland.

From Avondale, the southward road goes through the **Vale of Avoca,** passing the Meeting of the Waters, all made famous in the song of Thomas Moore. The next town, **Arklow,** is a busy little port with a boatyard where the finest ocean-going yachts in the world are built by a small family firm.

South of Arklow, head for **Gorey** and **Courtown** and thirty miles of quiet country roads between green hedges until you meet the main road again just north of Wexford. Thatched houses abound and every few miles a tempting signpost directs you a mile or two down the road to some hidden sandy cove and the sea.

On the main road near Wexford town look for a signpost to the **Wexford Wildlife Reserve,** the winter home of many thousands of wild duck and geese which come in from Canada, Greenland and even from Siberia. In summer plenty of duck and swans remain, and some of the rarer winter birds are kept in pens.

The final part of the journey from **Wexford** to **Rosslare** brings you through an extraordinary corner of Ireland, a flat region which in some ways seems to belong more to Holland and even has a windmill. The main road to Rosslare is easy to find, but you might take one more diversion before making your way to the

ferry port. The signposts are quite helpful, but there are a great many small roads and the best way to navigate is to bring the half-inch map Sheet 23 which shows all of them. I think there are more castles in this region than anywhere else in Ireland: they seem to appear behind every second hedge: some ruined, some still inhabited and a few even serving meals and welcoming guests.

The windmill, built in 1846, is at the village of **Tacumshane** and the other outstanding place to visit is **Lady's Island Lake,** where thousands of people go on pilgrimage every year. Our Lady's Island is a great green sward with a crazy ruin of a castle which leans even more than the Tower of Pisa. The island spends most of its time nowadays securely joined to the shore. The lake is an oddity in itself: every so often the sea throws up gravel which blocks the lake's outlet so that the water floods the surrounding land. Then the barrier is bulldozed away and the floods recede till next time.

From Lady's Island and its placid lake, a few short miles between the hedges and castles bring you back to the world of today. •

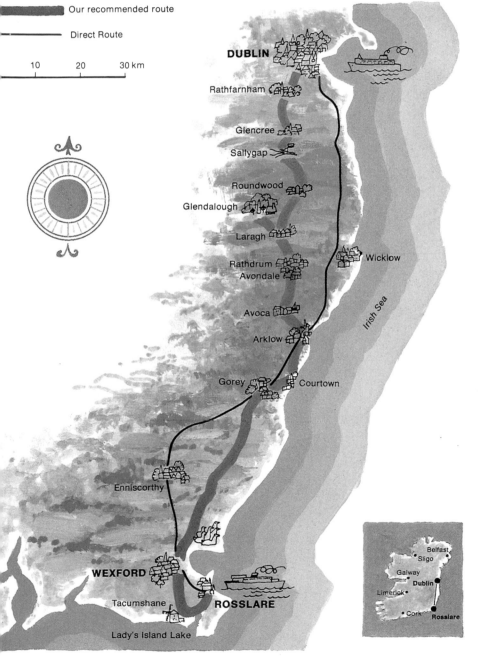

| Distances | miles | km |
|---|---|---|
| Dublin — Sallygap | 16 | 26 |
| Sallygap | 17 | 27 |
| Glendalough — Arklow | 21 | 34 |
| Arklow — Courtown | 14 | 22 |
| Courtown — Wexford | 28 | 45 |
| Wexford — Rosslare | 18 | 29 |
| Total | 114 | 183 |

## 38 DUBLIN TO LIMERICK

*Highlights. Blessington*, a village with old-world charm and many pubs and eating places and access to a beautiful man-made lake. *Russborough House*, a magnificent 18th century mansion with a fabulous collection of old masters. The *Curragh*, where they have been holding horse races for more than a thousand years, and *Kildare*, with an ancient round tower and a fine cathedral. *Emo Court*, another 18th century mansion with a lovely garden. *Slieve Bloom Mountains* with enticing deep and hidden valleys. *Birr Castle* with gardens, and the remains of one of the biggest telescopes ever built. Finally a drive with a view of *Lough Derg*, among the most beautiful lakes of Ireland.

*This is a long, lazy way of going to Limerick from Dublin, generally avoiding the direct route which is one of the busiest in Ireland. The country is gently hilly nearly all the way and the byroads have to twist and turn. The soil is rich so that there are many large farms and estates with green pastures and beautiful horses and old trees.*

Distances

|  | miles | km |
| --- | --- | --- |
| Dublin — Blessington | 18 | 29 |
| Blessington — Mountmellick | 38 | 61 |
| Mountmellick — Portumna | 39 | 63 |
| Portumna — Killaloe | 28 | 45 |
| Killaloe — Limerick | 20 | 32 |
| **Total** | **143** | **230** |

# DUBLIN to LIMERICK and SHANNON AIRPORT

*The road between Dublin and Shannon is probably the most traversed road in Ireland. It's fast enough (though Ireland doesn't go in much for six-lane highways) but you'll enjoy this alternative route much more, starting off on the road to Blessington.*

I met a policeman in **Blessington** who told me with great pride and pleasure that very little had changed in that village since I first visited it forty years ago. That might not be much to boast about until you reflect that Blessington lies just half an hour's drive from the centre of Dublin

and a quarter of an hour from one of the newest and biggest suburban townships.

The road to Blessington is a good one, but it doesn't lead directly to any large towns so it is pleasantly free from traffic. It climbs up and along the outer edge of the Wicklow hills, with a fantastic view behind of the fertile plains of Kildare and Meath and, on a clear day, the far-off Mountains of Mourne.

Blessington itself is an ideal village, neatly planned by good landlords of past generations and centred around

a church, a courthouse and a few bigger houses. One of these, by the way, is a delightful family hotel where you might stop for a cup of morning coffee — that is, if you are not tempted to spend the next few days there. If you have the time you can take a long drive around the **Blessington Lakes**, a trip which brings you far into the mountains.

But if you really do want to press on for Limerick and the southwest, go straight through the village, passing over an off-shoot of the lakes and maybe stopping at **Russborough**, one of the greatest of the great Irish houses and the home of a fabulous collection of European paintings. A little way past Russborough, take the

right turn which brings you through **Ballymore Eustace**. Like Blessington, it is a place apart but the contrast between the two villages is amazing. Blessington was planned and set out

in order along the sides of a straight road. But Ballymore just grew, with people planting houses anywhere they could so that the village runs untamed amongst the hills.

Westwards of Ballymore Eustace is the village of **Kilcullen**, straddling the River Liffey — and a place where you can buy the finest of hand-made saddles. Then you reach the **Curragh of Kildare**, a great rolling plain of sheep pasture, quite different from any other part of the Irish landscape. The town of **Kildare**, at the edge of the Curragh, was a monastic city from the time of St. Brigid who died early in the 6th. century. The **round tower**,

built a thousand years ago, can still be climbed and there is a marvellous view from the top. But on the other side of the road a signpost directs you to the **National Stud** and the **Japanese Gardens**. There you can feast your eyes on some of the world's most valuable racehorses or enjoy the harmony of an expatriate piece of Japan.

Just for a few miles after Kildare you stay on the main road, before going through **Monasterevan** and turning right for **Mountmellick**. There are many hotels on that road, but my preference is to bring my own picnic meal and stop in a forest near the

village of **Emo**. A signpost in the village saying **Emo Court** shows the way, and a drive of a mile or so into the wood leads to a clearing where you can rest among the trees, look at the wild flowers which grow among the rocks of an old quarry and listen to the birds singing. If you follow the road on through the forest you come to a mansion with gardens which you are welcome to visit. One of the fea-

tures of the park is an avenue of giant redwood trees, imported from California a hundred years ago.

Back to Emo village you continue westwards, soon reaching the edge of the **Slieve Bloom Mountains** where Fionn MacCool, the mythical Irish

hero, was brought up and where, a little more than two hundred years ago, the last Irish wolf was hunted and killed. Between Mountmellick and **Birr**, wonderful roads lead up into the mountains, twisting and turning to bring you around the deep gorges of the River Barrow and its tributaries. One of the finest leads from Clonaslee towards Mountrath and back to see the marvels of Birr.

Two wonderful things happened in Birr in the middle of the 19th. cen-

tury. One was the creation of a lake and a magnificent garden. The other was the construction of the biggest telescope in the world. Built in 1845 it remained the largest until 1917. The tube of the telescope, made from wooden staves, still lies there, the centrepiece of an open-air museum.

It is very difficult to decide where to go from Birr. You must see **Lough Derg**, one of the biggest and most beautiful of the lakes of Ireland. The problem is to make up your mind which side of the lake to travel. The shorter way goes to **Portroe** and leads to a lakeside park at **Castlelough**. The longer one crosses the Shannon upstream and passes **Portumna Forest Park** where there are deer and wild duck and walking trails through the wood and down to the lakeside.

Both roads lead to **Killaloe** with its hotels, cathedrals, boats by the hundred and the site of the palace of the great king Brian Boru. If, by this time, you have forgotten that you were heading for Limerick nobody would blame you. But it is only another twenty miles down the river.•

Portumna

Birr

Mountmellick

Monasterevan

Slieve Bloom Mountains

Roscrea

Portlaoise

Curragh

Kildare

Kilcullen

DUBLIN

Blessington

Ballymore Eustace

*Blessington Lakes*

——— Direct Route
▬▬▬ Our recommended route

0   10   20   30 km

# INDEX

# The Book of the Liffey: from source to the sea

*Edited by Elizabeth Healy, with texts by Christopher Moriarty, Gerard O'Flaherty and others*

*Awarded the Books Ireland medal for general books*

'Rarely can a river of eighty miles offer so much for discovery from its peaty birth-pool to its industrial harbour.'
A detailed, illustrated account of Anna Livia and its hinterland — its flora and fauna, folklore, history and literature, geology and geography — from boghole source to industrial harbour. Lavishly illustrated with over 200 maps, photographs, prints and drawings. A rare treat.
192 pages / Large format / Hardback / £16.95

'Beautifully designed' *Sunday Press*
'A pleasure to read' *Books Ireland*

# Down the Dodder

## WILDLIFE, HISTORY, LEGEND, WALKS

*Christopher Moriarty*

The story of the river and a detailed walker's guide, tracing the course of this river through the beauty of Dublin county and the bustle of Dublin city. In deepest suburbia, kingfisher and heron thrive, and foxes prowl the Dodder banks. In the city, shoals of mullet disport themselves. Wild flowers abound. The very stones tell of ice fields and of coral reefs. From the days when Oisin and St Patrick argued on its banks to the watermills of the nineteenth century and the first engineers working at its source to install Kippure television mast, the Dodder has a story to tell. , Christopher Moriarty reveals the wonder of legend and wildlife it truly is.
'Intimate and interesting ... every school and household along the river should have this book'
*Sunday Independent*
Colour and b/w photographs, maps, drawings and diagrams
200 pages / Hardback £12.95 / Paperback £8.95

# On Foot in Dublin and Wicklow

## EXPLORING THE WILDERNESS

*Christopher Moriarty*

46 walks of various lengths and difficulty, for ramblers, hikers, children and dogs in and around Dublin and Wicklow. Each route has a map, a history of the area and special features — dolmens, castles, wildlife, plants, rock formations — which add the excitement of discovery to the walk.
'It's a gem of a book at only £4.50 and brings sweetly to life some of the city's most cherished haunts.'
*Evening Press*

96 pages / Paperback / £4.50

# Our Way of Life

## HERITAGE, WILDLIFE, COUNTRYSIDE, PEOPLE

*Edited by Desmond Gillmor*

'It's the most thorough, multi-dimensional overview which reveals the vastly rich treasure which is ours in our countryside.'
This accessible, richly-illustrated book examines the Irish countryside and provides an understanding of our way of life. It explores the rich heritage of our past, our natural resources, conservation and environment, archaeology, land, work and recreation. Fully illustrated with line drawings and colour photographs.
Large format / Paperback / £12.99

**From your bookseller or from WOLFHOUND PRESS, 68 Mountjoy Square, Dublin 1.**
*Write for our catalogue.*